HISTORY *in* 30*Days*

GENESIS TO REVELATION

Blessings!

HIStory *in* 30 Days

Genesis to Revelation

WITH DAILY DEVOTIONALS

Carole O. Schryber

TATE PUBLISHING
AND **ENTERPRISES**, LLC

Published by Tate Publishing & Enterprises, LLC
127 E. Trade Center Terrace | Mustang, Oklahoma 73064 USA
1.888.361.9473 | www.tatepublishing.com

Tate Publishing is committed to excellence in the publishing industry. The company reflects the philosophy established by the founders, based on Psalm 68:11,
"The Lord gave the word and great was the company of those who published it."

Book design copyright © 2015 by Tate Publishing, LLC. All rights reserved.
Cover design by Norlan Balazo
Interior design by Shieldon Alcasid

Published in the United States of America

ISBN: 978-1-68187-097-7
Religion / Biblical Meditations / General
15.07.16

To John
My husband, best friend, and the smartest man I know

John, thank you for sharing your wisdom and knowledge as I prepared my original speech on this topic and then translated it into book form. You entertained countless questions on theology and history—at all hours of the day and night. Thank you to my children, Ben, Ricki, and Jack, for graciously allowing me to tell some of their personal stories. You learned long ago that your lives aren't very private! To my dear friend, Dee, thank you for helping me reshape the contents of my speech into book form. Your many hours of editing, phone conversations, and e-mails did not go unnoticed. You shared my enthusiasm for the project and desire to share God's story with others. Both you and John kept me on track when I was prone to change direction and lose focus. I know that was often a difficult task.

I also want to thank Michelle Buckner, who originally gave me this topic to speak on, and all those who listened to my speech and encouraged me, particularly Nicole Atkins, Norah Molnar, and Sue Moye. A special thank you to those friends who read the HIStory and devotionals in the early stages and provided valuable insight—Donna Gilbert, Karen Dodd, Kim Kloster, Natalie Walkley, and Kristy Whitsitt, and to those who prayed and encouraged me—the "meddling moms" (Chris Bush, Karen Dodd, and Susan Chagares), my precious Community Bible Study sisters, and my extended family—my parents, Nicholas and Anne Orzio, Lisa Camia, Sue Schryber, Rick Schryber, Wendy Schryber, Jim and Lynn Robbins. To my dear friend, Holly Leachman, whose mentoring and friendship over the years have encouraged me with her wisdom such as, "It is never too late to do the right thing"—thank you. You are all incredible blessings to me.

Contents

INTRODUCTION

A few years ago, I was asked to speak at a women's conference on the topic of *Genesis to Revelation* and my talk could only last sixty minutes. The Bible is long. The challenge was daunting. I speak rapidly, but how could I speak *that rapidly?* Even if I could speak fast enough to mention each of the Bible's sixty-six books in sixty minutes, how could I impart anything of substance? I reflected on what the Bible is. The Bible isn't a random collection of unrelated books. Rather, it tells one story from beginning to end. There is one plot throughout. Many of us are so accustomed to moving around in the Bible that the fact it's one linear story, threaded throughout, can get lost. Each of the sixty-six books carries the plot forward. For my talk, I highlighted the plot points from each book of the Bible. In this way, the audience could see the Bible as one story.

In this story, we see that God had a plan from the beginning to send us a Savior, His Son. Once we understand God's purpose in sending His Son, we can begin to seek the answer to the questions: Do *I* need a Savior? Where do *I* fit into God's story? His story is for us and about us—more specifically, it's about our relationship with Him. If we come to believe this is a story of nonfiction, authored by God, it should change the way we live.

I continue to give this talk to women's groups. And it's through that effort I came to be interested in writing this book. The book is divided into thirty days with each book of the Bible included. Each day gives you a part of the plot of the story—or HIStory—as I call it. While it's meant to be read daily over the course of a month, I realize that might not always be possible. Perhaps you'll need to skip your reading time here and there. If you do, return to read where you left off—reading each day in order. That will help you to see how the story unfolds.

I encourage you to find a quiet part of your day, perhaps the first ten to fifteen minutes before your morning rush begins. I hope you'll read with an open heart and believe this is God's story written for you. I recommend you start by asking God to reveal Himself to you, read the HIStory, read that day's devotional, and then end with the prayer. It's my hope that you'll carry with you throughout the day what the Lord has put on your heart.

For it's an AMAZING story.

Note: There is symmetry between the Old and the New Testament despite its not being recorded chronologically. The Old Testament begins with the history of God's people. It's followed by the writings of wisdom and literature and concludes with writings of the prophets. The New Testament begins with the history of Jesus Christ, the Savior. It's followed by the writings and letters of the apostles and concludes with a prophetic word—Revelation. For the purpose of seeing the Bible as one story, however, I've presented the HIStory primarily in chronological order. Every book from Genesis to Revelation is mentioned.

DAY 1

IN THE BEGINNING

HIStory begins…

"In the beginning, **God**…" Before there was anything—there was **God**. And not just God, but one God in three forms. **GENESIS** records that man was created in *our* image. There is a plurality to God—Father, Son, and Holy Spirit, which will be further revealed as the story unfolds.

In the beginning, God created. Out of nothing, He created, and He created by speaking. From God's mouth came all of creation. He created the heavens and the earth. He created light. He created the sky, stars, oceans, land, and vegetation. He created animals, including the creatures of the sea, birds of the air, and creatures of the land.

And after everything, God saw that it was good. Everything God created was good. There was nothing bad and nothing evil. And all of this came about because God spoke.

But God had more to do. He wanted something to demonstrate and witness His glory, provide fellowship, and rule over the rest of creation. To do all this, He created man. He wanted man to be in His image, though not necessarily physically. God would manifest Himself in different forms in Scripture through His attributes: the ability to communicate, think, reason, act, and love. While there was only one God—creator, omnipotent, and sovereign—man was created to share His attributes.

And man was distinguished from the rest of creation. He was not created from nothing, but from the dust of the ground. God Himself breathed into man's nostrils the breath of life, and man became a living being who would soon be called Adam.

God is good, and He didn't want Adam to be alone. Adam would need a helper. He'd need someone to come alongside of him to rule over the rest of creation. He'd need someone with strength and discernment. God paraded before Adam all the animals to name, but from these animals, no suitable helper was found. So from the rib of Adam, God created a woman who would soon be called Eve. She would be bone of his bones and flesh of his flesh. She'd be his helper. She'd live with Adam in this Eden. And while they couldn't create something from nothing, they were given the means to procreate.

God was pleased—*it was indeed very good.* God wanted man and woman to live for eternity with Him, without shame or guilt and without evil. And though they were naked, they felt no shame.

Devotional: Where Are We in HIStory?

"So God created man in his own image, in the image of God he created him; male and female he created them." Genesis 1:27

Twenty years ago, I was running errands in the car. While at a stoplight, I turned around to my four-year-old son Jack in the backseat. At that moment, the sun was beaming off his sweet little face.

"Jack," I said, "You have the most beautiful blue eyes."

And Jack responded, "Mommy, God colored me good."

God did indeed color Jack good. He colored us all good. He created man and woman. He did this not because He needed Jack or me or you, but to be a witness to His glory. We all exist wholly because of Him. Understanding God's purpose in making me, as well as every other individual in the world, is awe-inspiring. Each individual is able to reflect His image in different ways. How we reflect Him—with our thoughts, our communication, and our love—will be unique.

Jack, in his innocence, was speaking a truth we as adults sometimes forget. We are here solely because of Him. In the beginning, God created.

Today I Pray

Lord, thank You for giving me life. As I go through my day, I pray I'll be mindful of Your amazing creation.

Day 2

THE ORIGINAL SIN

HIStory continues…

Adam and Eve lived in ideal conditions in the Garden of Eden where their every need was fully met. God's will for them was to live in paradise with Him forever. As God walked and conversed with them, He had one command:

"…You may surely eat of every tree of the garden, but of the tree of the knowledge of good and evil you shall not eat, for in the day that you eat of it you shall surely die" (Genesis 2:16–17). This was the first of several covenants God gave to man. It was conditional. Follow Me and you will live; reject Me and you will die. Adam and Eve had a part to play in this covenant. God asked for obedience, but He gave Adam and Eve the ability to *choose* obedience.

Why did God allow Adam and Eve to choose whether or not to be obedient? Because choosing obedience to God would demonstrate "relationship" and demonstrate that Adam and Eve trusted God even as to things they didn't understand. Disobedience to God would give them knowledge of what is outside God's will, and what is outside the will of God is evil. God wanted Adam and Eve to be holy, as He is holy.

Adam and Eve weren't alone in the Garden. Satan, in the form of a serpent, was there. God didn't create Satan as evil. God created him as a good angel in the heavens who could follow God's will. But Satan had chosen separation from God. There in Eden, Satan wanted to tempt Adam and Eve to disobey God and thereby gain the knowledge of evil. Satan lied and tricked the woman. He misquoted God's command. Even though God hadn't given Adam and Eve a reason not to trust Him, Satan's intention was for man and woman to doubt God's goodness and to make them believe that God was withholding something from them. Satan tempted them into believing that if they ate of the tree of the knowledge of good and evil, they would be "like God." They would have the same wisdom as God, so they wouldn't need God. The trust relationship would be broken. Satan tempted them, saying:

"...You will not surely die. For God knows that when you eat of it your eyes will be opened, and you will be like God, knowing good and evil" (Genesis 3:4–5).

"Oh, to be like God," Eve perhaps thought! It wasn't good enough to believe God and trust Him when He said there was something called evil. Eve disobeyed. She questioned God—the same loving God who'd given them everything in the Garden of Eden. God's perfect will for man and woman was that they'd never disobey. But God's permissive will was to give them the choice of obedience and life. The story of Adam and Eve demonstrated that even with the abundance in paradise, man and woman chose not to obey God.

Adam and Eve ate the fruit. Sin is the choice to know evil or that which is against God's perfect and holy will. The source of their sin was pride. They felt they deserved more.

In the moment they disobeyed, guilt flooded into them for the first time, and it separated them from God. The perfect image of God was scarred. Adam and Eve hid from God. Much as disobedient children might hide from their parents in shame, Adam and Eve covered their naked bodies in shame. Yet their covering, fig leaves, was inadequate to make atonement for their disobedience.

Devotional: Where Are We in HIStory?

"For all have sinned and fall short of the glory of God."
Romans 3:23

My parents have told me that as a small child I was fascinated with our electric stove. I loved to watch the coils go from black to red and then to black again. Of course, my mother and father told me repeatedly not to touch it. They didn't make this household rule to be unkind or to withhold something valuable from me. They didn't want me to experience the pain of touching the hot stove. They wanted me to trust them. Their love for me set the limit.

Essentially, God told Adam and Eve not to touch the hot stove. He wanted them to never experience pain or evil but to know it existed by their trust of His word. Despite His abundant love and perfect provisions for them, Adam and Eve didn't trust God's word. It was their *choice* to disobey that caused their suffering and separation from God. We may blame them for the consequences that God imposed on mankind, but are we so sure we wouldn't have made the same decision? How long would I have gone without scarring God's perfect and holy image? One day, when my mother wasn't looking, I touched the stove. I burned the entire palm of my hand.

Aren't we still faced with the same basic choice that God gave to Adam and Eve? How often do we choose to follow our own desires rather than trust His word and direction? Do we always humble ourselves and realize that God knows what's best for us? Or do we make decisions based on pride—thinking we know best? In one sense, it should be easier for us to choose what's good. Adam and Eve had never experienced evil. We have. We know what it is, and yet we still choose to depart from what we know is righteous and holy. Can we really say that we choose to be in God's presence every moment of every day? How confident are we that we would have resisted, for eternity, that other voice rather than heed the voice of God? Despite His loving warning, how often do I still touch a hot stove?

Today I Pray

Lord, I confess that sometimes rather than accepting Your loving warning, I too follow my own desires. I pray to receive the boundaries You set with a grateful heart.

Day 3

SEPARATION FROM GOD

HIStory continues…

Like a good and loving parent would know, there had to be punishment for sin and consequences for disobeying God. Love requires justice. Yet before God enumerated the consequences, He demonstrated grace to humankind. He cursed Satan: "…on your belly you shall go, and dust you shall eat all the days of your life. I will put enmity between you and the woman, and between your offspring and her offspring" (Genesis 3:14b–15a).

The dictionary defines "enmity" as a feeling or condition of hostility or hatred. God promised that hatred would arise between the serpent and the woman. Satan would be allowed to exist in the world as a despised creature, and he'd tempt the descendants of woman. There would always be a battle between them—for goodness and evil can never reconcile. Had God stopped there, the future would have been discouraging and hopeless for man and woman. But God continued with a promise of destruction to the serpent.

God gave just a glimmer of His grace and plan to rid the world of evil and destroy Satan. "…He shall bruise your head, and you shall bruise his heel" (Genesis 3:15). The promise seems vague, but it will be further explained as the story unfolds. Essentially, it was a promise of a Savior. Who would this "he" be? This is the first reference to a hero of the story. The "he" would be an offspring of Eve who would bruise the head of the offspring of the serpent (Satan). The word "bruise" is rendered from the Hebrew word "crush," which means to break into pieces or greatly injure. The head is a vital organ and, when crushed, is fatal. Satan would be destroyed. The Savior would have his "heel bruised." A bruise to the heel isn't fatal. The Savior would live.

There would come a time when the enmity would no longer exist. God, through our "bruised" Savior, would deem us to be without knowledge of evil. Relationship with God would be restored. While we're not told the specifics in Genesis of how this would happen or which offspring of Eve would be the Savior, God told us there would be a happy ending. God had set in motion a plan of hope, the promise of a Savior—a hero unlike any other.

God then enumerated the consequences to Adam and Eve for their sin. Eve now had pain in childbirth and Adam had to toil hard. Adam and Eve couldn't eat from the tree of life and live forever. They'd both suffer and ultimately experience a physical death and return to dust. Man and woman now knew evil by the pain of experiencing it. The loving God had wanted them to be spared that pain by trusting Him, but Adam and Eve chose disobedience. Finally, until their physical deaths, they'd experience a spiritual death—a separation from God. No longer would God walk with them in the garden. They were banished from the Garden of Eden. From that moment on, all humans had sin born into them. The children of Adam and Eve and all their descendants were no longer reflections of the image of God—love, joy, and goodness in its purest form. That image was scarred, and Adam and Eve would bear children in their own sinful image.

God's punishment didn't cause this spiritual death. The spiritual death was a result of sin and sin itself creates a separation from God. Adam and Eve demonstrated this by their desire to cover their naked bodies out of guilt and shame. But God is loving and gracious, and from the beginning, He provided a means for temporary reconciliation with Him.

An animal was killed, and God Himself made garments of skin for Adam and Eve to cover their nakedness and shame. God provided the means of atonement. God established that an innocent animal would have to die as a substitute to atone for the sin of man and woman. It would be the blood from that animal that would reconcile man with God. Killing an innocent animal wasn't a cruel act of God. Life is in the blood, and the visual of seeing the blood was to show man and woman that their selfish act was so serious as to cause death. The death of the animal was meant to teach them about the cost of sin.

The scarred image of God was evident through Eve's first offspring. She gave birth to Cain and Abel. Abel's sacrifice, made with faith, was the blood of a firstborn innocent animal. This was pleasing to God. Cain's sacrifice, made without faith, was the fruit of the land. This was not pleasing to God. Cain was jealous that God favored Abel's sacrifice. The first murder was committed when Cain killed Abel. Sin breeds more sin.

Devotional: Where Are We in HIStory?

"By faith Abel offered to God a more acceptable sacrifice than Cain, through which he was commended as righteous, God commending him by accepting his gifts. And through his faith, though he died, he still speaks." Hebrews 11:4

My husband and I were young parents when we decided that perhaps we should start going to church. Neither of us had any prior interest, but we thought it would be good to raise our children with some exposure to religion. We began attending various churches to find one that fit much like one might try on different shoes. Our criterion was simple—we wanted to feel good. One of the first churches we attended failed our test. The pastor began talking about sin; specifically, he referenced sins that I was all too familiar with. Of course, at that time, I didn't acknowledge them as sins. That would have required an acceptance that many of the things I'd done in my early years were against God's standards. We left that church. I refused to return. In fact, because of my stubbornness, we didn't attend church for a couple more years. Why was I so stubborn?

It was both a lack of faith in God's forgiveness and my pride that kept me from looking at my sins as sins. A relationship with God requires that we acknowledge we're sinful and have, by our choices, caused a separation from our Creator.

Today I Pray

Lord, today I will tear down the wall that separates me from You by acknowledging my sinfulness. I ask that You release me from my guilt and shame.

Day 4

GOD FAVORS NOAH

HIStory continues…

As man and woman multiplied, they became increasingly wicked: "The Lord saw that the wickedness of man was great in the earth, and that every intention of the thoughts of his heart was only evil continually" (Genesis 6:5). Humans had become so depraved. "And the Lord regretted that he had made man on the earth, and it grieved him to his heart" (Genesis 6:6).

God chose to send rain to destroy those who sought the knowledge of evil. He would leave an indelible mark indicating that the wages of sin is death. It would have been easy for God to wipe out everyone and begin again, but God demonstrated that redemption was available for the righteous. It was another picture of God's grace.

One man, Noah, had found favor with God. Noah walked with God, not perfectly, he was sinful, but he sought to do the will of God. Noah was told to build an ark when it's possible that it had never rained. He obeyed and built the ark in the precise dimensions God commanded. Noah preached to the people, but they didn't heed his warning. God gave the people a veritable lifetime to turn to Him during the many years the ark was being built. Finally, the doors of the ark closed. It was too late to board, and the floods came. The time of God's mercy was over. Noah's family was in the lifesaving boat. The rest who didn't seek to follow God were outside of the boat. At any earlier time, the people could have entered. Like Adam and Eve, they heard the word of God and chose to reject it. This was also a foreshadowing of a future time, when it would be too late to receive God's salvation for eternity.

Because Noah's family was saved, at the end of the flood, they were given responsibility for governing the world for God. God had preserved a people. The promise of a "bruised" Savior from Eve's offspring was preserved. The Savior was still to come.

God gave a sign of His peace and grace—the dove. Noah made his sacrifice at the altar, and God promised that never again would He cover the earth with a flood. He marked this covenant with a rainbow.

But a cycle, begun with Adam and Eve, would be repeated over and over through history. Man and woman would sin, God would judge, blood would have to be shed to remind man and woman that their sin had consequences, God would forgive, then God would give a sign of hope. His grace would restore and redeem when the people couldn't rescue themselves. God would preserve those who walked with him.

Devotional: Where Are We in HIStory?

"...Noah was a righteous man, blameless in his generation. Noah walked with God." Genesis 6:9

When our children were young, my husband continually told them to "dare to be different." Often, they didn't want to hear this. They didn't want to dare to be different. They wanted to be just like the other kids. They wanted to see adult-themed movies if the other kids were seeing them. They wanted to play inappropriate video games if the other kids were playing them. With regard to inconsequential things, my husband would respect their choices. But still he would remind them to dare to be different. He said it would train them for the things that mattered. Living a life in accordance with God's holy standards requires boldness.

Noah made the choice to live righteously when everyone around him chose to do evil. Noah was not without sin, but he had a heart for God and a desire to walk with Him. God continues to make a way for the righteous to walk with Him. It begins, however, with the bold willingness to build the ark and get on, despite what the world thinks. It requires a willingness to follow His standards rather than what the culture says is right.

Today I Pray

Lord, I want to dare to be different—to live according to Your righteous ways. Help me to see that Your ways are better than the ways of the world.

Day 5

ABRAHAM IS CHOSEN

HIStory continues…

During the many years that followed, the population grew. God hadn't forgotten His promise that **one** from the offspring of Eve would destroy Satan. How would this **one** be identified? There were, after all, a lot of people born from Eve's lineage. God would want this Savior to be recognized. So God selected one man, Abraham, from Eve's lineage. It would be through Abraham that we could trace the offspring going forward.

He was a man with nothing, and yet it would be through him that God would expand the promise to send a Savior. Abraham was a nomad living in the land of Ur when God called him to leave his homeland and travel to a place that God would show him. Abraham obeyed, and God made a covenant with Abraham that had several components:

1. A promise of a *people*: Abraham would be the father of a great nation.

2. A promise of a *land:* Abraham was promised the land upon which Abraham was standing—the Promised Land. It would belong one day to His, to God's, chosen people. (God planned this as a foreshadowing of a future place for God's people.)

3. A promise of a *blessing*: Through Abraham the nations of the earth would be blessed.

This was a unique covenant. Only one party was necessary. It had no conditions. It wasn't dependent on anything Abraham or his descendants did or did not do. Unlike the covenant that God had made with Adam that had the condition "do not eat," God alone would keep this covenant with Abraham. This would be part of the plot, and the fulfillment of the covenant would unfold in the pages of the Bible.

God made this covenant not because Abraham and his offspring were better than anyone else or more deserving. As stated previously, Abraham and his offspring were chosen so we could identify the promised Savior when He came. Abraham's family would also be witnesses who could testify and record all that God did. This would provide the evidence to link the Savior with the promise of the covenant. To the world, it would seem like an impossible promise to keep. Abraham and his wife, Sarah, were very old when God made this promise. How would Abraham have descendants as numerous as the stars? This made no more sense to Abraham than God's statement to Noah to build an ark.

While Abraham had moments of impatience—for God made him wait—he believed. And finally, Sarah had a miracle baby in her old age. Witnesses would have to think: "It must have been God" to give a baby when it was scientifically impossible. The Bible records many instances where God performs a miracle so that the people will know that He is God. This miracle would also foreshadow the birth of the future Savior, whose birth would also be scientifically impossible.

Abraham continued to walk with God in obedience. Yet as righteous as Abraham was, he wasn't without sin. Sin separates us from a holy God. To atone for sin, a sacrifice had to be made to God. On one occasion, God tested Abraham's obedience. He asked Abraham to offer up his son, Isaac, as a sacrifice. Abraham trusted God. He knew God would somehow keep His promise of numerous descendants, and therefore, in faith, Abraham brought Isaac to the altar. Abraham told Isaac that God would provide a lamb for the sacrifice. Abraham and God were so close, and yet how painful it must have been for Abraham to walk up the mountain, prepared to sacrifice his beloved son Isaac. Just as Abraham was about to strike Isaac, an angel stopped him. A ram—caught in thorns—was in the thicket. The ram took the place of Isaac and became the blood sacrifice to cover Abraham's sin. Abraham called this place, "the Lord will provide." Certainly, Abraham knew the Lord had and would always keep His promises.

Devotional: Where Are We in HIStory?

"And he [Abraham] believed the Lord, and he counted it to him as righteousness." Genesis 15:6

Remarkably, Abraham was prepared to give his son as a sacrifice to the Lord! How was he able to demonstrate such faith? Abraham must have learned much about God through his past journeys. Despite moments of Abraham's disobedience, God had continually kept His promises and protected Abraham. God had proved Himself faithful. All that Abraham learned about God over the years was stored in his heart and mind, so at a time that could have been Abraham's most tragic hour, he could trust God. He didn't need to know *how* God would provide. He just needed to know that God *would*. How can we cultivate this level of faith?

When my mother-in-law lost her husband to bone cancer, she grieved his absence tremendously. They did everything together, and she missed him. Shortly thereafter, she herself got cancer. With courage, she faced a painful battle. After she passed, I was cleaning up her things and found a bag containing all her medical records and insurance information. I felt sad. It reminded me of our many times together during the last year of her life. That bag had gone with us to every medical appointment. As I went to discard it, I felt something at the bottom. It was a small well-worn journal held together with rubber bands. Inside, written in her own handwriting, was verse after verse of Scripture. There were verses of comfort from the Psalms, verses of the promises of heaven, and verses of God's character of love. While she'd made a few journal entries reflecting on her pain in losing her husband, the journal was primarily a remembrance of all she knew to be true of God. This was how she'd persevered through the dark hours of her grief.

What we learn about God from praying, reading the Bible, and memorizing Scripture *today* can prepare us for pain ahead. During times of suffering our emotions and anxiety can take over unless we hold on to what we know is true: God loves us and has a plan for our lives. He has given us the means to obey even during the hard times. Like Abraham, in order to endure the trials of this world, we need the knowledge of God and His promises.

Today I Pray

Lord, I pray for a longing to read Your Word daily, so that I might know You and Your promises for my life.

Day 6

JOSEPH SHOWS FORGIVENESS

HIStory continues…

Abraham knew that God would keep His promise of blessing the world through Abraham's descendant. The promise to bless was somehow tied to a blood sacrifice that God would provide. One day, an innocent intervener, wearing His own crown of thorns, would emerge as the sacrifice to atone for all the sins of man once and for all. Because the promised descendant and Savior would need to be recognized, the lineage of Abraham had to be carefully recorded.

Abraham's son Isaac had two sons, Esau and Jacob. While the two were still in the womb of Rebekah, Isaac's wife, they struggled with each other. The Lord told Rebekah that these twins would grow into two nations that would always be divided. God also told Rebekah that the older twin would serve the younger. And just as God had foretold, when Isaac was dying, his younger son, Jacob, deceived his father into bequeathing the "blessing" to him rather than to the oldest son, Esau.

The blessing would be more than a material blessing. It would mean that God's promise to Abraham would pass through Jacob, the younger. It seemed incredible that the promise would be fulfilled through a deceitful man. Yet one night after Jacob wrestled with God, he subordinated his own will to God's. Afterward, God renamed him "Israel," which means one who "reigns with God." This was an illustration for future generations. When God's people have an encounter with Him, a transformation takes place. The descendants of Isaac's son Esau would be the Edomites. They would choose to battle with Israel for generations.

Jacob (Israel) had twelve sons who represented the twelve tribes of Israel. Joseph was the youngest son of Israel. His jealous older brothers resented the favor their father showed Joseph and plotted to get rid of him. They sold him into slavery in Egypt. Though Joseph endured many trials as a slave in Egypt, he remained true to God, praising Him for all things. Eventually, Joseph found himself before the pharaoh. The pharaoh found favor in Joseph—such that he appointed Joseph to a high position in the Egyptian government. Joseph was credited with saving Egypt from a famine. The famine also devastated Israel. But God's providence intervened to protect Abraham's descendants.

Because of Joseph's high position in Egypt, he was able to provide food to the brothers who had betrayed him. Without Joseph's grace, God's people would have perished, and God's promise wouldn't have been kept. God's people would always need saving. Joseph would also serve as a picture of the Savior to come, whose grace and mercy would be extended to sinful and undeserving people.

Devotional: Where Are We in HIStory?

"But Joseph said to them, 'Do not fear, for am I in the place of God? As for you, you meant evil against me, but God meant it for good, to bring it about that many people should be kept alive, as they are today. So do not fear; I will provide for you and your little ones.' Thus he comforted them and spoke kindly to them." Genesis 50:19–21

Like Joseph, we're called to forgive. And like Joseph, we never know when God has a plan that He can execute only if we've forgiven someone who has trampled our hearts.

My father grew up with a dad who rejected and abused him repeatedly throughout his life. How understandable it might have been if—at best—my father deserted his dad or—at worst—sought revenge. But instead, he ultimately made the decision to overcome his feelings of pain and forgive his father. When my grandfather was elderly and in need, his son lovingly cared for him. Isn't it possible that God used these circumstances to soften the heart of an old bitter man before he died?

Loving the offender is an act of obedience and thankfulness to God. Sometimes we're so overwhelmed by the wrong done to us, we fail to remember that God can use those circumstances for His purposes. We can demonstrate His mercy by forgiving. It's a choice we make because God first loved us. Could I have forgiven as Joseph did?

Today I Pray

Lord, help me to forgive those I hesitate to forgive. I pray that I can show mercy as Joseph did.

Day 7

CALL OF MOSES

HIStory continues…

God's people multiplied. (God's promise to Abraham of a *people*.) They resided, however, in Egypt. How would God keep His other promise? (God's promise to Abraham of a *land*.) Genesis ended with the death of Joseph in Egypt. Joseph was a man of faith. Before he died, he made his sons promise that one day his bones would be moved from Egypt to the Promised Land. He knew all God's promises to Abraham, including the one of land, would one day come to pass.

Genesis demonstrated that the people God created would sin. The enmity between Satan and the offspring of Eve would continue. Man and woman would choose not to follow God. And yet God had already set in motion a plan to redeem them and to reconcile His sinful people to Himself. (God's promise to Abraham of a *blessing*.)

The story continues in **EXODUS.** Within four hundred years after Joseph's death, the descendants of Abraham in

Egypt were so numerous they were perceived as a threat to the dictatorial power of the existing pharaoh. The pharaoh responded by enslaving God's people. Despite this enslavement, the population continued to grow just as God had promised. The more they were oppressed, the more they multiplied. So the pharaoh came up with another plan. He instructed the midwives to kill the newborn boys of the Israelites. When the fear of the God of Israel prevented the midwives from carrying out the pharaoh's command, the pharaoh then ordered that every boy born to God's people be thrown into the Nile. This plan, if successful, would have extinguished the descendants of Israel. God's promise to bless the world with a Savior from the offspring of Eve and from a descendant of Abraham would have been thwarted.

God needed to rescue His people once again. For this purpose, He selected Moses. Though Moses was one of the newborns sentenced to death by the pharaoh, he was saved. His mother placed him in a basket that she floated down the Nile. It was the pharaoh's own daughter who retrieved the basket from the Nile, rescued Moses, and raised him as her own. Moses grew to become a proud leader in the Egyptian military before God revealed to him his true heritage. Moses was called to rescue the people of God.

At first, he attempted to rescue the Israelites without God's help. Moses was appalled to see one of his people being physically abused by an Egyptian. Impulsively, Moses intervened and killed the Egyptian. When the pharaoh heard this, he wanted Moses killed. Moses became a fugitive living in exile. Without God, he demonstrated he was powerless.

Forty years later, God appeared to Moses in the burning bush and again called him to rescue the Israelites out of Egypt. A humbled Moses declared: "…Who am I that I should go to Pharaoh and bring the children of Israel out of Egypt?" (Exodus 3:11). God's answer to Moses's doubt was to remind Moses that He, God, would be with Him. The people would be saved not through the strength of Moses, but through the work of God. God further declared: "…Say this to the people of Israel, I AM has sent me to you" (Exodus 3:14).

Devotional: Where Are We in HIStory?

"When the Lord saw that he turned aside to see, God called to him out of the bush, "Moses, Moses!" And he said, "Here I am." Then he said, "Do not come near; take your sandals off your feet, for the place on which you are standing is holy ground." And he said, "I am the God of your father, the God of Abraham, the God of Isaac, and the God of Jacob." Exodus 3:4–6

As a law student lacking in humility, with lofty ideas of rescuing women via my law practice, if someone had said I'd give up the law and instead teach women's Bible study, I'd have thought them crazy. But God has a plan for our lives. He can overcome every objection or obstacle if we're obedient. God can get us from A to B to C if we just wait for His call and His timing.

His timing for me meant leaving my job, relocating to a new state without friends or extended family for support, three children all under the age of six, and a husband with overwhelming work hours.

I sought out the companionship of other women in a Bible study group. This led to becoming a small group leader, then an assistant teaching director, mentoring young women seeking God, and now full-time women's ministry. In the end, God indeed did have a plan for me to work with women but not in the way I had once envisioned.

Moses had been a man with a great reputation—raised by the pharaoh's daughter in the government palace. But God didn't call Moses because of his stature in the community. He called Moses because he was ready to submit to God. It would not be Moses's own plan that would rescue the people; rather, it would be through God's plan.

Today I Pray

Lord, I want to be obedient. If my way is not Your way, help me commit to Your plan for my life. Give me the patience, also, to wait on Your perfect timing.

Day 8

THE PASSOVER LAMB

HIStory continues…

Moses confronted the pharaoh: "Let my people go!" But the pharaoh refused. God sent a series of nine plagues on Egypt, each time requesting that the pharaoh let His people go. The nine plagues might seem to the outside eye to be random, but they weren't. Each plague attacked or mocked one of the Egyptian gods. For example, Hapi was a frog goddess of the Egyptians. God sent millions of frogs as one plague. The Egyptian people were helpless to do anything about this plague. They couldn't kill the frogs because they'd be killing their god. The Egyptians depicted both their god Apis and the goddess Hathor as cattle. One plague caused the death of livestock as a judgment against this god and goddess. Through the plagues the God of Israel was shown to be more powerful than any of the many gods of Egypt. They were idols—but He is God. God is still more powerful than any idols of this world.

God sent nine plagues to force the pharaoh's hand, yet God's people remained enslaved. The pharaoh was given many chances to obey God by releasing the Israelites. Each time he refused to obey, his heart hardened, until ultimately, God gave him over to his hardened heart. Then the Lord said to Moses: "Pharaoh's heart is hardened; he refuses to let the people go" (Exodus 7:14). Finally, God said the firstborn sons in all Egypt would die, which would fall on God's people as well. God couldn't let that happen. His people would again need saving.

God showed what it took to be saved from death. He told His people to take a lamb, kill it, and put some of the blood on the top and on both sides of the doorframe to their home. When God saw the blood on a house, He would "pass over" that house, and the firstborn would live. The "blood of the lamb" would be attributed to each person who applied it. Escaping death was not dependent on how *good* one was. Escaping death was dependent on how *faithful* one was. Only by accepting God's protection in faith could they be saved.

This was another foreshadowing of the Savior who would come—the Passover Lamb—whose blood would be shed like the ram substituted for Isaac, so that *eternal* death would be *passed over*. The people would continue yearly to celebrate the *Passover* by a sacrifice of an innocent animal. This was in remembrance of God's mercy and grace and what He did for them on that night. He and He alone saved them.

Devotional: Where Are We in HIStory?

"Say therefore to the people of Israel, 'I am the Lord, and I will bring you out from under the burdens of the Egyptians, and I will deliver you from slavery to them, and I will redeem you with an outstretched arm and with great acts of judgment. I will take you to be my people, and I will be your God, and you shall know that I am the Lord your God, who has brought you out from under the burdens of the Egyptians." Exodus 6:6–7

The judgment on the Egyptians was God's way of demonstrating that He wanted a relationship with His people. He wanted them to know what He could and would do for them. He didn't want them to just *know of* Him. He wanted them to *know Him.* There is a great distinction between knowing God exists and actually knowing Him. If I were to show you a picture of my husband, John, you'd be able to recognize him if he came in the room. You might say, "That's John Schryber." You might even be able to recount certain things you'd heard about him—that he's a lawyer, that he has three grown children, that he loves the St. Louis Cardinals! But you couldn't say, "I know John Schryber." That would require more than seeing his picture and knowing a few facts about him. That would require having a relationship with him.

God's desire was to have a relationship with the Israelites. If He intervened in their lives by rescuing them from bondage, and if He kept His covenant with them, they would begin to know Him in a personal way. They would want to worship and serve Him. Therefore, before every plague, God gave the pharaoh the reason He wanted them to be free. It wasn't just to have a nice home, a prosperous life, and freedom from the pain of slavery. God said: "Let my people go so that they will serve Me." In some translations of the Bible, it's "so they will worship Me."

God's purpose for freedom was spiritual, not physical. It was to be in personal relationship with Him. By demonstrating His power and releasing them, His people would truly know Him as God and desire to be in His presence and serve Him. It was—and still is—God's desire that we know Him, not just know of Him.

Today I Pray

Lord, I confess I've failed to take the time to really know You. Forgive me. I have faith that You will reveal Yourself if I will just seek You.

Day 9

THE TEN COMMANDMENTS

HIStory continues…

God heard the cry of His people and in His grace released them from their bondage. They left Egypt with the Egyptian army pursuing them. When the Israelites came to the Red Sea, with one last miracle, God parted the Red Sea and His people passed through and were rescued. They were then brought to new life on their way to the land that God had promised. Moses met with God on the other side of the Red Sea in Sinai where God established a new order.

God's first covenant, with Adam, had one condition—don't eat the fruit. The Abrahamic Covenant had no conditions and contained God's promises to Abraham—a people, a land, and a mysterious blessing. Now God gave Moses a new covenant that had ten conditions—the Ten Commandments. This covenant was a standard of perfection for God's people and a standard of obedience that God wanted them to meet. The law was to set God's people apart and, through obedience, mark them as His

Holy people. It should be remembered that keeping this Mosaic Covenant wouldn't alter the original promise made to Abraham. God would always keep that unconditional promise. The Ten Commandments were part of a conditional covenant. By obeying the laws, God would bless His people, and it would go well for them.

But God knew that His people wouldn't be able to keep the law perfectly. They'd depart from it time and time again. *Why then did He give it?* In one sense, the law was meant to be a mirror. The people would see in it how far they could depart from the image of God—his blueprint. It was meant to show the Israelites how sinful they were and to reveal the condition of their hearts. But a mirror can only reflect. We don't use mirrors to clean our faces. We need a cleanser for that. God's people, every man and woman, would need a cleanser to rid them of dirt. God revealed in the commandments more of his created intent. The law was meant to show the people how desperately they needed a Savior—a sacrifice—to wash away their sin.

Israel would become God's evidence to the world of His power and His control. If they obeyed, there would be blessings. If they disobeyed, there would be judgment. And it would all happen as God said. It was one thing to establish a plan to redeem; it was another thing for the people to see that they needed the plan at all. God wanted His people to recognize their need for the Savior. Their continual disobedience would accomplish that. If in order to approach God, they needed to obey the law perfectly, then no one—no earthly being—would be able to approach God. The law would demonstrate this, and therefore, God would continually require a blood sacrifice to atone for the people's sins.

The prideful Israelites, however, thought they could do it. They accepted the law rather than cry for mercy. In fact, they responded: "…All that the Lord has spoken we will do." (Exodus 19:8) They believed they could please God on their own, thinking: "I can do this. I can do enough good works. I can be good. I can be perfect." The remainder of the Old Testament illustrates how Israel failed to follow God's perfect law.

Devotional: Where Are We in HIStory?

"Moses came and told the people all the words of the Lord and all the rules. And all the people answered with one voice and said, "All the words that the Lord has spoken we will do." Exodus 24:3

I recently read that there is an app for Macs and PCs that blocks social networking sites such as Twitter and Facebook. If you have to get work done, the app takes away your distractions for a designated period. Technology gurus have realized that we need to be saved from ourselves! God, of course, knew this from the beginning. He gave the law to show the Israelites that on their own they'd be distracted by the world and couldn't keep God's holy standards.

When we think of the original Ten Commandments, we may feel as confident as the Israelites did when they said they could fully obey. After all, most of us can claim that we've never murdered, committed adultery, or even stolen property. We feel confident we can control our actions. However, if we're truthful, can any of us say we've never struggled with the last commandment? *Thou shall not covet.* This includes a command not to covet (envy or strongly desire) *anything* my neighbor has—my neighbor's house, car, new kitchen, her well-behaved children, her job, or even her gifts and abilities. (She sings beautifully and I can't carry a tune.) Each time we covet, we depart from God's perfect standard. We're essentially saying that what He has blessed us with is not enough, and we know best. The root of covetousness is pride and a focus on our selfish desires. The commandment not to covet forces us to search our hearts, as well as our actions. We may be able to fool the world and appear fully righteous, but God sees us. Knowing He sees my disobedience makes me realize that I, too, need a Savior.

Today I Pray

Lord, help me to overcome the sin of envy. I pray I can replace envy with a heart full of gratitude for all that I have.

Day 10

CALL TO WORSHIP

HIStory continues…

God gave the law—the Ten Commandments—and Exodus records that He also provided a place His people could meet with Him. It was to be the *tabernacle,* a tent that would move with the people as they traveled to the Promised Land. It was to be constructed exactly as God prescribed. Later, a structure, the *Temple,* would be built in Jerusalem with the same physical components as the tabernacle. Both the tabernacle and the Temple symbolized God's presence and would be temporary provisions for God's people. They were a foreshadowing of a permanent dwelling place for God. Someday, God would dwell in the hearts of man and woman.

God is holy and His presence requires the cleansing of sin. God gave man and woman this opportunity. Within the tabernacle, and later the Temple, the high priest made a sacrifice by substituting the life of an innocent unblemished animal in exchange for the sin of man and woman. As the people would continue to sin, the blood of the innocents would be shed over and over again. God wanted them to see that their sin had grave consequences—it separated them from Him. While this was God's temporary plan and provision for reconciliation, it foreshadowed the hope of a permanent atonement. One day, Satan would receive the fatal bruise to his head through the sacrifice and suffering of Eve's offspring, a Savior, who would come through the line of Abraham. Evil would be banished, as God had intended.

It was in **LEVITICUS** where God established that the people would need an intercessor, or high priest, to approach God on their behalf and to make their sacrifices. The priest would come from the tribe of Levi. Of course, there was a problem. The priests themselves were not without sin and would first have to make atonement for their own sins. An imperfect priest was a temporary provision that pointed to the promise of a perfect high priest to come—one without sin. God reminded His people they were to worship Him. Those redeemed, those who atoned through the system of sacrifice, could come into His Holy presence.

The promises of God had to be fulfilled. After all, God promised. So where are we in God's plan? The people had escaped Egypt, they were numerous, but they didn't yet possess the land that God had promised. The Land of Canaan was in the possession of pagan nations. The Israelites needed to travel from Sinai to Canaan. During this time, the people demonstrated that they still couldn't keep the law, they were complainers, they were rebellious, and they didn't respond to God's grace with gratitude. On their own, they couldn't approach God. But God faithfully led them as they continued on their journey to the Promised Land.

In the book of **NUMBERS,** we read that when they were on the brink of the land God had promised to Abraham, they sent out spies to look over the land they would possess. Two spies, Joshua and Caleb, claimed the land to be ready for God to take. But ten of the spies reported giants in the land. The people were overwhelmed and afraid, agreeing with the majority that it was too dangerous to enter. Because of their unfaithfulness, God ordained forty years of additional wilderness wanderings for His people. Only the two obedient men—Joshua and Caleb—would be allowed to enter the Promised Land with the next generation.

Devotional: Where Are We in HIStory?

"Then all the congregation raised a loud cry, and the people wept that night. And all the people of Israel grumbled against Moses and Aaron. The whole congregation said to them, "Would that we had died in the land of Egypt! Or would that we had died in this wilderness! Why is the Lord bringing us into this land, to fall by the sword? Our wives and our little ones will become a prey. Would it not be better for us to go back to Egypt?" Numbers 14:1–3

At this point in the story, the Israelites are worshiping God in the tabernacle. They knew that God created the heavens and all that was in the earth, knew that He had wiped out the world with a flood, knew that He had sent numerous plagues that covered Egypt, and knew that He had parted the Red Sea and led them out of bondage. Yet despite their knowledge of Him, they panicked over a few giants in the land. By letting their fears take over and forgetting what He had done in the past, they reduced the size of their God. How often do we, today, reduce the size of God?

I know of all the great miracles recorded in the Bible. I've personally witnessed miracles in my life and in the lives of others. At times when I'm tempted to be anxious or panic, I, too, need to remember God's sovereignty.

When my son Ben was nineteen years old, he spent a summer studying in China. He'd finished exams and he and a friend were planning to leave Shanghai and go to Thailand for two weeks. That morning, Ben woke me with a phone call at 6:00 a.m. (6:00 p.m. in China). Ben was terribly sick. He had food poisoning. He'd already been to a hospital, received an IV of fluids, been released—but he was still very ill. I told him he should go back to the hospital and skip his Thailand trip, if necessary, and we'd arrange for him to come home. Ben agreed. We said goodbye. This was before our phones had international calling capabilities—he'd called from a borrowed phone. Fifteen hours later, I still hadn't heard from him. I was a wreck. Was he in the hospital, had he recovered and gone to Thailand, or was he dead! These are the thoughts of a parent.

I decided I had to find him. I had no leads as to which hospital he'd gone to. I entered "Shanghai hospitals" into my search engine and hundreds came up. I randomly picked one, connected to an international operator, and called. My husband thought I'd lost my mind. Did I really think I could find Ben? The first receptionist that answered spoke very little English, and she gave me another number to dial.

"Do you speak English?" I asked the woman at this new number.

"A little," she replied.

"I'm looking for my son who was very sick and went to a hospital in Shanghai," I continued.

"Ben?" she asked. I almost fainted.

"Yes," I answered.

"I will connect you with the ER nurse."

Within one minute, I was speaking to a woman who explained that Ben had returned about fourteen hours earlier. They gave him another IV, antibiotics, pain medication, and dismissed him after several hours. My heart rested. The next day, Ben called from Thailand apologetically. He hadn't had phone access. He had no idea what he'd put our family through.

How did a distraught mother find her son in a foreign city with hundreds of hospitals and just two phone calls? I need to remember that I have a BIG God.

He's still the same God the Israelites had come to know and the God capable of the same miracles. What problems do we have that God can't resolve? Certainly, He doesn't always answer in such clear terms, but I believe He has revealed enough of His capabilities for us to recall them during times of uncertainty.

Today I Pray

Lord, thank You that You are a BIG God—the God of the Israelites. Today I will recall a time when, despite my doubt, You rescued me.

Day 11

JOSHUA NOW LEADS

HIStory continues…

In the book of Numbers, God recounts the wanderings of His people. The people continued grumbling about their circumstances. Moses became angry with them, but rather than trusting God to deal with His people, he sinned and disobeyed God. Therefore, God determined that Moses would not lead the people into the Promised Land.

As righteous as Moses was—he was, after all, a deliverer of his people—he wasn't the *one* promised. What better way to demonstrate that he wasn't the promised Savior than to forbid Moses from entering the Promised Land? God chose Joshua, instead, to lead the people. Moses gave a wonderful encouraging speech to the people to again remind them of God's promise of future blessings. It's recorded in **DEUTERONOMY.**

God's promises were still preserved. A descendant of Abraham would one day bless the nations of the world. In order to recognize Him and in order to prove that He was the promised Savior, the genealogical record of Abraham's family would have to be kept. It was.

The history of God's chosen people continues with Joshua leading the people into the land, so the second of God's promises to Abraham would be kept. God vowed that He would be with Joshua on this journey: "Have I not commanded you? Be strong and courageous. Do not be frightened, and do not be dismayed, for the Lord your God is with you wherever you go" (Joshua 1:9). God would always be with His people.

God led the people across the Jordan River and into the Promised Land. Because the land was occupied by pagan nations, the Lord directed Joshua in several military campaigns to take over the land. His protection was obvious. One of the most well-known instances called for Joshua to lead a march with trumpets around the city of Jericho for six days. On the seventh day, the walls of the city came down and God's people were able to capture the city. God's direction and Joshua's obedience are recorded in the book called **JOSHUA.**

The land was not yet fully conquered near the end of Joshua's life. In faith, however, Joshua divided the land between the tribes of Israel, with the exception of the priestly tribe of Levi. The designation was the recognition of their inheritance and God's promise of land. The descendants of Joseph, the favored son who rescued the people many years earlier, were given two shares of land represented by his two sons. The tribes were commanded to conquer the pagan people occupying the land. God would give them victory if they obeyed Him. As God's people entered and overtook the various nations, He wanted them to rid the land of the pagan and evil practices. He wanted them to worship Him alone. Life in this land wouldn't be easy for God's people, but God again promised blessings for obedience and consequences for disobedience.

Under the leadership of Joshua, the people of Israel served the Lord and not idols. And just like Joseph, the bones of Joshua were buried in the Promised Land. Joshua was the model of a faithful servant of God. Before he died, Joshua reminded the people of God's Mosaic covenant and the personal choice each could make. God made it clear, as He did in the Garden, that man and woman had free choice, and the freedom to choose the consequences of serving self rather than God.

Devotional: Where Are We in HIStory?

"...But as for me and my house, we will serve the Lord." Joshua 24:15

This verse is painted above our front doorway. As we pass it to go from room to room or when we leave to go out into the world, it reminds us whom we're called to serve. Sadly, we need the reminder. Joshua was a faithful servant who knew the insidious danger of worshiping idols. As the Israelites entered and mingled with pagan nations, the temptation would be too great to turn their hearts from God and serve foreign idols. The same temptation still exists. Our foreign gods may not be gold statues, but they're real nonetheless. The world worships material goods and success, education, power, celebrities, good looks, and a host of other things. How can I recognize if I'm serving another god?

Do I want success in business more than integrity? I'm serving the god of power.

Do I want approval from my peers more than to live by God's holy standards? I'm serving the god of popularity.

Do I spend my money first on entertainment and material items and give God what is left over? I'm serving the god of money.

Do I focus on my children's accomplishments over their spiritual condition? Perhaps I've made my children my idols.

Fortunately, it's never too late to serve God and God alone. As Joshua also commanded the Israelites, "…choose this day whom you will serve…" (Joshua 24:15) I have a choice each day to serve God.

Today I Pray

Lord, I choose to be a faithful servant who serves only You. Please give me the strength to resist worldly idols.

Day 12

RUTH CHOOSES GOD

HIStory continues…

The government in the new land was a theocracy. God was their ruler, guide, and king. God gave the people judges, righteous men who would lead as the people began to occupy the Promised Land. Life under the judges is recorded in the book named **JUDGES.**

The events of Judges demonstrated the cycle of sin. As soon as a judge died, the people would again disobey. God would then punish the Israelites by delivering them into the hands of a different nation. That would lead to repentance, and God would ordain a new judge. There were thirteen cycles of this and a total of fourteen judges. It's quite tiresome reading this account of the people. Why couldn't the Israelites learn from their past sins?

God was showing them that they couldn't approach Him on their own. God wanted His people to realize they were to be a people set apart—holy—and separate from the pagan practices of the world. He would always have this same desire for His creation. Yet again and again, they were disobedient. They always needed rescuing.

The story of **RUTH** is the story of one life under the rule of the judges and another story of redemption. Ruth was from one of the pagan nations, Moab. The Moabites worshiped the pagan god, Chemosh. Historical records indicate that this god required such practices as human sacrifice. His very name means "destroyer." During a famine in Israel, a man and his wife, Naomi, along with two sons went to live in Moab. After the man died, his sons married Moabite women, Ruth and Orpah. After about ten years, the sons also died. Without a husband or sons, Naomi chose to return to her people when she'd heard there was no longer a famine. Ruth chose to accompany her mother-in-law back to the land of God's people. Ruth pledged to worship the God of Israel and her faithful service was blessed. She married Boaz, a wealthy Israelite, who is part of the line of Abraham. Ruth would become the great-grandmother of King David. It would be from the line of David that God would further identify the *one* promised long ago. And the Savior would come from the offspring of Ruth.

Devotional: Where Are We in HIStory?

"…Your people shall be my people, and your God my God. Where you die I will die, and there will I be buried. May the Lord do so to me and more also if anything but death parts me from you." Ruth 1:16–17

Ruth had a sister, Orpah. They both were Moabites and their husbands were Naomi's sons. When their husbands died, the natural choice would have been to return to the land of Moab where they had family and friends. Ruth insisted, however, on following Naomi and was blessed for her choice. Orpah returned to Moab and is never referenced again in the Bible. What compelled Ruth to make the harder choice to follow Naomi into the unknown?

Ruth decided that Naomi's people would be her people. In other words, she chose a family. There was something about her mother-in-law she was drawn to. When my husband and I were first dating, I felt drawn to his mother. She was a follower of Christ. I wasn't a follower of Christ at the time and I recognized in her something that I didn't have. She seemed to always have joy—even during times of difficulties. She lived her life with humility. My husband still jokes that I fell in love with his family before I fell in love with him. That may be an exaggeration, but I must admit I wanted to follow his mother and be part of her family.

The next component of Ruth's decision was a choice of God—your God shall be my God. This was quite a commitment on the part of Ruth. It's one thing to love someone and feel an obligation of loyalty that leads to following that person. It's quite another thing to change the god you worship! What did Ruth know about the God of Naomi that made her willing to worship Him instead?

Had she learned from Naomi that He was a God of love and mercy? Had she learned from Naomi that He was more powerful than any of the pagan gods? We don't know, but we do know that she knew enough about Him to surrender to Him. The book of Ruth is a wonderful story of God's redemption and blessing to a woman who made a bold walk in faith.

In the early years of my marriage, I began to learn about the God my in-laws worshiped. It would take me several years more to make the commitment Ruth made, but I began a journey to know the same God. Who we follow matters. As God's story unfolds, we see that the choice we make determines our eternal destiny. Orpah could have chosen as Ruth did. But the pull of her past life, and the god she was familiar with, was too great. The sisters had access to the same knowledge and chose different paths.

Today I Pray

Lord, I pray I can be a Naomi to a Ruth. I pray Godly attributes will flow from me and encourage others—that they might desire to know "my" God.

DAY 13

SAUL IS KING

HIStory continues…

The last judge was Samuel. There are two books of this history named for him—**I and II SAMUEL**. Samuel was not only a judge but also a prophet of God.

The Israelites became dissatisfied with the theocracy God had established. Essentially, they declared—*We want to be like everyone else.* The rest of the nations had kings. The Israelites wanted to unite all the tribes as one nation under the rule of a king. God's desire was that they be distinguished from the other nations. It wasn't that God objected to a new system of government for the people—He would soon select a human king of His choosing for them—but He wanted them to wait on His timing. God's desire for them would be that they worship Him and seek guidance from Him alone. And He wanted their human king to submit to His authority. God would be King of kings. Unfortunately, the Israelite's demand for a king demonstrated that they didn't want God to rule over them at all.

Though God warned them, through Samuel, that a king wasn't a good idea, in His permissive will He honored their request. God had one provision—worship Me and Me alone. All would still be well in the land if the people and their king worshiped Him. If they didn't, there would be judgment and consequences for turning away. (Again, nothing would affect the unconditional promise to Abraham of *a people, a land,* and *a blessing.*)

Saul, the first king of the Israelites, was strong, handsome, and from a good family. He wasn't "humanly" inferior, quite the opposite. God gave the people what they wanted—a king like the world's kings. But Saul didn't seek God's direction and purpose. From the beginning of his monarchy, he and the people didn't honor God. Samuel tried to warn Saul, but his warnings were ignored and the Israelites suffered due to Saul's sinfulness. God was demonstrating that His blessings would only come from obedience.

Devotional: Where Are We in HIStory?

"...But there shall be a king over us, that we also may be like all the nations, and that our king may judge us and go out before us and fight our battles." 1 Samuel 8:19–20

The Israelites declared their reason for wanting a human king. They wanted a king to judge them rather than God. Sadly, I understand this, for I lived many years rejecting God's reign for the same reason. It's much easier to live according to the world's standards than by God's holy standards. The worldly view has no absolute standard of right and wrong. We can convince ourselves that any behavior is justified.

With society as my judge, I could justify any behavior that was popular at the time. By convincing myself that my choices were okay because they were culturally acceptable, I made the world my king. It was much more fun to "be like all the nations." But the pleasure was always short-lived. Often, I was left feeling alone and full of guilt. The world couldn't provide comfort or release my shame. Israel found that life under King Saul's rule proved to have grave consequences for years after his reign.

God wants to be our judge and protector. He wants us to live according to His standards of holiness. When we do, we can be assured of His blessings of peace and joy that surpass the fleeting pleasure that comes from pursuing earthly passions.

Today I Pray

Lord, I pray for the strength to reject my desire to "be like other nations." I ask You and You alone to reign over my life.

Day 14

DAVID IS ANOINTED

HIStory continues…

The second king was David, chosen by God's prophet Samuel. David was the eighth and youngest son of Jesse from the tribe of Judah. By the world's standards, the fact that David was the youngest son and was also a shepherd would have seemed to make him a surprising choice. Although chosen by God's servant, the path to kingship wasn't easy for David. For more than fifteen years God trained David through many trials and tribulations. King Saul wasn't going to give up the throne without a fight, and David became a fugitive, fleeing in order to escape Saul's wrath. David had the opportunity to kill Saul, but waited for God's timing to become king.

After the death of King Saul, David was anointed. He first ruled over just the house of his own tribe and later over all Israel. During the period of King David's reign, the nation flourished and conquered its enemies. Israel became the envy of the nations surrounding it.

David was the primary author of the **PSALMS.** Throughout his songs, he expressed his honest fears of danger during his trials, but he boldly declared that his only hope was in God. David was far from a perfect man. He committed adultery with Bathsheba and then murdered her husband. He always repented and grieved over his sins. He expressed his desire that God search his heart: "Search me, O God, and know my heart! Try me and know my thoughts! And see if there be any grievous way in me, and lead me in the way everlasting!" (Psalm 139:23–24). So God, who looks on the heart of man, referred to David as "a man after God's own heart."

From David's lineage, God would further narrow the promise made hundreds of years earlier to Abraham. Through the prophet Nathan, God promised David: "When your days are fulfilled and you lie down with your fathers, I will raise up your offspring after you, who shall come from your body, and I will establish his kingdom. He shall build a house for my name, and I will establish the throne of his kingdom forever" (2 Samuel 7:12–13).

David was a foreshadowing of the Savior to come. God had promised that the Savior would come from the offspring of David, from the line of Judah, and one day, He would reign forever.

Devotional: Where Are We in HIStory?

"The Lord is my shepherd; I shall not want. He makes me lie down in green pastures. He leads me beside still waters. He restores my soul. He leads me in paths of righteousness for his name's sake. Even though I walk through the valley of the shadow of death, I will fear no evil, for you are with me; your rod and your staff, they comfort me. You prepare a table before me in the presence of my enemies; you anoint my head with oil; my cup overflows. Surely goodness and mercy shall follow me all the days of my life, and I shall dwell in the house of the Lord forever." Psalm 23

David's life was full of suffering. For long periods, he lived and wandered alone, hiding from his enemies. He endured struggles and was the object of jealousy from King Saul as well as from his brothers. And yet he sang: "The Lord is my shepherd; I shall not want." David used his times of suffering and failure to get closer to God.

In my community, Jill's House is an overnight care facility for children with intellectual disabilities. It's a ministry started by my church, and its doors are open for any family, regardless of religious background. It gives parents a much-needed respite to rest and recharge. Last year, I was asked to lead a Bible study for the parents. They were invited to come to learn about the Christian faith. I didn't know what to expect, nor did I know what, if any, background they had with Christianity. I spent a considerable amount of time preparing an "intro" curriculum that would address some relevant issues. I also prepared in hopes of answering tough questions that might come up, particularly about the authority of the Bible as the Word of God. As it turned out, the parents were the ones giving the lessons. Their curriculum had come from life.

It didn't take long to discover that every parent in attendance had a deep faith in God—not because they hadn't wrestled with doubt—but because they had. They openly and honestly shared past struggles and the hard questions they'd asked of God over the years.

Each parent could testify that suffering and failure were opportunities to draw close to God. It was in the valleys that they learned that God is real. I'd come prepared with much evidence to support why I've come to believe in God and His Son, the Savior. But their evidence was powerful and irrefutable. Their lives were the evidence.

Why did the parents come to the meeting? Perhaps it was to be in fellowship with others who know their problems. But I believe it was primarily their obedience to God. Like David, who declared his love for God in Psalms, these parents knew they had a story to tell that could benefit others. If they could find intimacy with a personal God and experience His mercy and love in the midst of suffering, they knew that was worth testifying about.

Today I Pray

Lord, You are my shepherd; I shall not want. You make me lie down to green pastures. You lead me beside still waters. You restore my soul. You lead me in paths of righteousness for Your name's sake. Even though I walk through the valley of the shadow of death, I will fear no evil, for You are with me; Your rod and Your staff, they comfort me. You prepare a table before me in the presence of my enemies; You anoint my head with oil; my cup overflows. Surely goodness and mercy shall follow me all the days of my life, and I shall dwell in Your house forever.

DAY 15

SOLOMON NOW REIGNS

HIStory continues…

There was one last king of the united kingdom of Israel. He was David's son, Solomon. God had given Solomon great wisdom. While it's uncertain whether he wrote or merely collected the writings in **PROVERBS, ECCLESIASTES**, and **THE SONG OF SOLOMON,** the timeless wisdom recorded in these books of literature speaks of the benefit and blessings of relying solely on God for direction and instruction. "Trust in the Lord with all your heart, and do not lean on your own understanding" (Proverbs 3:5).

During Solomon's reign, the nation grew in wealth, and among other nations, it grew in stature. God ordained Solomon to build His Temple. It was erected in the exact specifications that God had commanded many years previously. Within the Temple was a large and heavy curtain that signified the separation of God from the people because of their sin. Beyond the curtain was the

Holy of Holies. Once a year, on the Day of Atonement, the high priest from the tribe of Levi entered the Holy of Holies and sprinkled the blood of a slain lamb on the altar of God, known as the Ark of the Covenant. The people would know that the innocent animal had died exclusively because of their sins, and it was through this blood sacrifice that their sins were forgiven. God in His mercy had granted a way for His people to atone for their sins and come into His presence.

As magnificent as this Temple was, it was merely a dim reflection of the permanent temple God would someday provide. After all, the Temple was built by man and could be destroyed, which it was several times during the course of Israel's history. And the sacrifice for atonement would have to be made repeatedly year after year. God planned for a future *forever* temple and a *permanent* sacrifice.

The enmity that God had ordained in Genesis between Satan and the offspring of Eve was apparent. Satan continued to tempt individuals into sin throughout the history of Israel. It was always God's desire that man and woman would stand strong and choose to obey Him out of love rather than to yield to the lies of Satan.

The book of **JOB** records one man's faith in the midst of Satan's attacks. While it's uncertain when during the history of Israel Job lived, he was a model of one who would hold true to God's commands, despite Satan's temptations. Satan took Job's property, took Job's children, inflicted Job with pain and illness. Yet despite all Satan did, he couldn't break Job's faith. Job's story is a picture of God's power over Satan. Job also prophetically looked forward to a time when the Savior would come. He declared: "For I know that my redeemer lives, and at the last he will stand upon the earth. And after my skin has been thus destroyed, yet in my flesh I shall see God" (Job 19:25–26). Job was a descendant of Abraham who witnessed and testified that God's blessings were to be eternal—there remained a promise that a redeemer would conquer death.

Devotional: Where Are We in HIStory?

"…Have you considered my servant Job, that there is none like him on the earth, a blameless and upright man, who fears God and turns away from evil?" Job 2:3a

The story of Job is difficult to read. God not only allowed Satan to take away everything from His faithful servant, but He even suggests to Satan that he test Job. We want judgment on evil people but not on someone like Job!

Shortly after I married, I witnessed my new in-laws go through a long period of trials. The house my father-in-law built and where they had raised their family burned to the ground. Shortly after rebuilding it, my father-in-law was diagnosed with cancer, and they began a different kind of battle. I couldn't believe their "bad luck." They were followers of Christ, and yet their lives weren't void of pain. While they shed many tears, through it all, my in-laws always thanked God for everything they still had. Just as Job's faith was never crushed, neither was the faith of my in-laws.

The purpose of following God is not just in hopes of being rescued from trials or to be spared from suffering. It'd be easy to follow God if He continually gave us only what we wanted. But true faith allows us to rely on God for peace regardless of circumstances and to trust God in all things, as Job taught us.

Today I Pray

Lord, I want Job's faith. Please guide me to a faith that is never crushed despite the trials I face.

DAY 16

THE DIVIDED KINGDOM

HIStory continues…

Each of the twelve tribes, which made up God's chosen nation, had descended from the sons of Israel (Jacob). Just as with squabbling children, the tribes often argued among themselves. God wanted them to be unified as one nation under His Kingship, but because of their continued disobedience to Him, the nation of Israel would one day divide. He foretold this through His prophet Ahijah.

In a display of God's sovereignty, the nations did divide after Solomon's death. Just as prophesied, a servant of Solomon, Jeroboam, was given authority to rule over ten of the northern tribes. Solomon's son, Rehoboam, became king over the southern two tribes of Judah and Benjamin.

The northern ten tribes became the nation of Israel. The two southern tribes became known as the nation of Judah. They were all God's chosen people, but sadly divided. The history of the divided kingdom of Israel is recounted in **I and II KINGS** and **I and II CHRONICLES**.

Under the leadership of many evil kings, both nations often worshiped idols and took on the pagan practices of the nations that surrounded them. The Temple was no longer the exclusive place of worship for God's people. Despite the continued disobedience, God warned them to return to Him. His grace was abundant, and He called them to repent time and time again through His spokesmen, the Major and Minor Prophets.

The prophets gave warnings of future judgment for disobedience as well as hope for redemption. The essential message to Israel and Judah was that they weren't to rely on their own strength, nor were they to make allies with the neighboring pagan nations. This had been the same message Moses had given to the people upon entering the Promised Land. God wasn't discriminating. This was to protect His people. The surrounding nations were evil, and God's eternal warning would be to reject the evil practices and idols of this world. God knew that if His people didn't separate themselves from the world, they'd become like the pagan nations rather than like God.

The prophets also foretold of three different future periods: (1) a *near future* time of captivity if the nations didn't repent, (2) a *more distant future* when the Savior would come to save them from their sins, (3) and a *far future* time when the Savior would return to establish His eternal Kingdom. The words of the prophets can be divided into the following categories: prophets to Israel (the northern kingdom), prophets to the surrounding nations, prophets to Judah (the southern kingdom) prior to exile into Babylon, prophets to Judah during their exile, and prophets to Judah after being released from exile.

The prophets Elijah and Elisha were faithful spokesmen of God who called the northern kingdom of Israel to turn their hearts to Him. Other prophets to Israel, with books named after them, spoke warnings of judgment.

AMOS condemned not only Israel's neighbors, but also Israel itself for violating God's laws. He warned the people that if they continued with the practice of idolatry and sinfulness, they'd be taken captive by the powerful and evil nation of Assyria.

HOSEA was the last of the prophets who spoke to the northern kingdom of Israel. While the other prophets emphasized power and justice as the essential characteristics of God, Hosea gave a picture of God's forgiveness for unfaithfulness. God would never forsake them, even if He allowed punishment.

Sadly, Israel didn't respect God's warnings, so as foretold, the nation of Assyria succeeded in taking Israel captive in 722 BC (2 Kings 17). The northern kingdom of Israel ceased and its people, who represented ten of the twelve tribes, were scattered outside the Promised Land. If God had promised that the Savior would come from one of the northern tribes, the fulfillment of His promise would have been impossible to verify. God, however, had promised He would come from the tribe of Judah, part of the southern kingdom.

Devotional: Where Are We in HIStory?

"The days of punishment have come; the days of recompense have come; Israel shall know it." Hosea 9:7a

When our son Ben was about nine, he and two friends were playing at our house. Our eight-year-old daughter, Ricki, was out at a sleepover with her own friends. We had a family rule that our children were to respect the property of one another. This included a restriction not to play in a sibling's room without permission. That evening, unbeknownst to me, the boys violated the rule by going into Ricki's room. As only young boys can dream up, they experimented by putting various liquid substances into the bowl of her beloved pet fish. The water changed color. The boys quickly decided they'd better clean out the bowl to remove the evidence. They took the fish out with a net, changed the water, and replaced the fish. They didn't know that putting this kind of fish back in very cold water from the tap could kill the fish.

The next morning, my daughter came home to find her fish floating in the bowl. She was distraught. "What are the chances he'd die on the one night I was out?" she exclaimed. As far as we knew, the fish had died of natural causes.

We had a burial in the backyard and Ricki gave a eulogy. Ben was silent throughout. Several days later, Ricki came home from school exploding with anger. The youngest of the boys, unable to hold the truth in any longer, confessed to her what they'd done. I immediately confronted Ben. With tears in his eyes, he confessed that they'd accidentally killed Ricki's fish. But I'll never forget what Ben also said: "I'm so glad you know the truth. I couldn't stand living with the secret for another day." Ben knew that his disobedience had created a barrier not only between his sister and him, but also between the two of us. He gladly accepted his punishment, which included using his own allowance to buy Ricki another fish.

God, through His prophets, had warned Israel repeatedly to repent and turn to obedience. They would always be God's people, and yet there could be no true fellowship with God as long as His people had unconfessed sin and lived in disobedience. Without punishment, it would be as if God were sweeping the sins under the rug. The punishment demonstrated His love and justice. In order to be true to His word, God had to discipline Israel.

Today I Pray

Lord, do I have any sin that I need to confess to You? I pray, as King David once did: "Search me, O God, and know my heart! Try me and know my thoughts! And see if there be any grievous way in me, and lead me in the way everlasting!"

Day 17

PROPHETS TO NATIONS

HIStory continues…

God warned the surrounding nations that there would be destruction if they were evil and brought harm to His people. He would hold the nations accountable, but He gave them opportunities to do what was right in His sight. Further, when His promises came true and were recorded in history, this would be evidence that God was the one true God. God demonstrated His sovereignty and His control of the destinies of every nation. We see in the words of the prophets that God didn't just come to save the Israelites, but the blessings were meant for all. Somehow, the promised Savior would bless everyone who received Him.

OBADIAH was sent to the nation of Edom (descendants of Esau). He foretold that their pride and cruelty against Israel would be their downfall.

God asked **JONAH** to preach to the evil Ninevites. However, Jonah was an Israelite and didn't like the idea that God was offering these evildoers, who had committed atrocities to his fellow people, a chance to repent. Jonah didn't want to offer them mercy. He wanted the people of Nineveh to be destroyed. Because of his disobedience to God, Jonah found himself thrown into the sea where he was swallowed by a great fish. Jonah called to God in his distress, and God rescued him after three days and three nights. Jonah was given a second chance to obey and he did. He went into Nineveh and preached of God's plan to overthrow the city if they didn't turn from their evil ways. The king and the people of Nineveh repented. God abandoned the disaster set to befall them. Jonah had done what God asked of him, but he was still angry with God for showing mercy to the Ninevites. But God demonstrated to Jonah that He pities those who don't know Him and wants to give all an opportunity to repent.

God in his mercy had spared this nation once after Jonah's warning, but it continued its practice of evil. Nahum the prophet was also sent to Nineveh with the message that God is slow to display His wrath, but that He avenges sin and unrighteousness. Nineveh is the capital of Assyria. The cruelty of Assyria is documented in the book of **NAHUM**, as well as in history. It's referred to as "the city of blood," with "many casualties, piles of dead, bodies without number, people stumbling over the corpses" (Nahum 3). The practices of the Assyrians were cruel. They skinned men alive, removed their tongues, and dismembered their bodies. The evil they inflicted on His people finally resulted in God's display of judgment.

God, through the prophets, made predictions regarding the surrounding nations if they didn't repent. It all came true just as he said. The history books record this.

Devotional: Where Are We in HIStory?

"Now the word of the Lord came to Jonah the son of Amittai, saying, "Arise, go to Nineveh, that great city, and call out against it, for their evil has come up before me." But Jonah rose to flee to Tarshish from the presence of the Lord. He went down to Joppa and found a ship going to Tarshish. So he paid the fare and went down into it, to go with them to Tarshish, away from the presence of the Lord." Jonah 1:1–3

When I read about the atrocities being committed by heinous terrorist organizations in the world, I cannot imagine offering them forgiveness. I want punishment and I want it now. It's okay for mercy to be extended to those who commit "minor" sins but certainly not to those who are EVIL.

Jonah felt that mercy should be reserved for the Israelites, and not the rest of the world, particularly those who harmed his people. They were terrorists. If he warned the Ninevites of God's anger, they might repent. If they repented, God might be gracious and forgiving. That could not happen! Even though Jonah had been extended mercy from God when he disobeyed (God rescued him from the whale), Jonah felt that the sin of the Ninevites was far too great to forgive.

However, throughout the history of Israel, God was demonstrating that mercy for one means mercy for all. That's why He sent prophets to the foreign nations. No one deserves mercy. Compared to God, we're all unworthy. When I compare my own sins against those of terrorists, I feel great about myself. But if I compare myself with God, I know that I'm a profound sinner. Instead of measuring my "goodness" against others, I need to compare myself with God's holiness. God continued to rescue Israel only out of His mercy, and He would continue to rescue anyone who called on Him, only out of His mercy. Moreover, God wants us to be merciful as He is merciful. That means telling everyone of God's love and forgiveness.

It's not our place to judge another. Our focus should be on recognizing our own sinfulness, making our own hearts right and pure and appreciating that we have a merciful God.

Today I Pray

Lord, help me to understand that You want everyone to repent and know You despite what evils he or she may have committed. Give me a merciful heart to accept Your will.

Day 18

PROPHET ISAIAH CALLED

HIStory continues…

The ten tribes living in the northern kingdom had been conquered. God's promise of a Savior coming from the lineage of Abraham would now have to be fulfilled through the descendants in the southern kingdom. There were only two tribes in the southern kingdom—Benjamin and Judah. God had earlier promised that the Savior would come from the tribe of Judah.

Kings ruled Judah at this time. The idea of worldly kings to govern the people was not God's perfect plan for them. Kings of the world couldn't be trusted. When these kings did evil in the eyes of the Lord, the people would stray and follow their earthly kings. God sent prophets to Judah in the southern kingdom to warn them to obey God. God wanted his people to turn to Him, to let Him alone rule their lives and nation.

Judah did have some obedient kings among those who ruled her who attempted to destroy idolatry and restore the worship God had commanded. When Assyria tried to overthrow Judah, God spared her because of the righteousness of King Hezekiah and the influence of prominent prophets. But His people were still sinful and there were consequences for her sin.

ISAIAH warned of Judah's captivity by the evil empire of Babylon if Judah didn't obey. He also prophesied that a man named Cyrus would subdue Babylon and let God's people be freed without any ransom paid. Isaiah made this prophecy 150 years before a Persian king named Cyrus was born.

The prophecies of Isaiah extended beyond the near future of God's people. More than any other prophet, Isaiah prophesied about the coming Savior and His Kingdom. The promise of Abraham was to be preserved. God, through Isaiah, gave greater indicators of how the Savior would be identified. For example, Isaiah said the Messiah would be born to a virgin and preceded by one who would call all to repentance.

Isaiah also gave specifics of how the Messiah would save. He would be a sacrifice, a suffering servant, who would redeem the people. He would be pierced for our sins (our transgressions). He would be mocked and flogged. He would suffer as He saved.

Isaiah described a Savior who would be more than a political or military conqueror. The Savior's mission would be for the purpose God set forth from the beginning, to reconcile man and woman with God. He—the Savior and Messiah—would take upon Himself our iniquities, and

He would receive the punishment on our behalf for our sins. He could only do this if He were Himself without sin. Isaiah makes clear that the coming Savior would be a sinless man who would suffer for the sake of the world.

Isaiah also looked forward to an eternal reign of the coming Savior: "For to us a child is born, to us a son is given; and the government shall be upon his shoulder, and his name shall be called Wonderful Counselor, Mighty God, Everlasting Father, Prince of Peace. Of the increase of his government and of peace there will be no end, on the throne of David and over his kingdom, to establish it and to uphold it with justice and with righteousness from this time forth and forevermore. The zeal of the Lord of hosts will do this" (Isaiah 9:6–7).

This passage illustrates that Isaiah looked forward to an everlasting reign of peace. But doesn't the history of the world tell us that peace is not possible with mere mortals in charge? We're called to combat evil. Our success, however, can only be limited because of the greed and hard hearts of political rulers, dictators, and terrorists throughout the world. So how could Isaiah boldly proclaim with confidence that one day there would be everlasting peace?

The peace that Isaiah foresaw would be ushered in by a different kind of king. After all, how could a mere mortal man reign forever? Isaiah's prophecy clearly stated that He would be human: "For to us a child is born…" However, in order to reign forever, He would have to be more than human. He would be Mighty God, Everlasting Father, and Prince of Peace! The coming Savior would come to us fully human and yet fully God. Only that kind of king could lead the world to peace. This knowledge gave Isaiah the boldness to profess truth to the world in face of evil.

Devotional: Where Are We in HIStory?

"Of the increase of his government and of peace there will be no end, on the throne of David and over his kingdom, to establish it and to uphold it with justice and with righteousness from this time forth and forevermore. The zeal of the Lord of hosts will do this." Isaiah 9:7

I first realized the world wasn't safe on the day Kennedy was shot. I was a young girl who up to that point was focused mainly on playing with my Chatty Cathy, riding my bike, and catching fireflies in a jar. Suddenly, things changed. If our president could be shot, are any of us really safe? My children's day of awakening was 9/11.

Fast forward to today. We can't turn on the television, read the paper, or even have a casual conversation with a neighbor without becoming acutely aware of the great depravity, injustice, and evil in our world. It's paralyzing.

Perhaps this is how Isaiah felt. But Isaiah knew and proclaimed that one day there would be a righteous ruler who would have the last word. Someday, this Savior-King would reign forever in peace.

Today I Pray

Lord, You know I'm discouraged when I see the evil in this world. Let me find comfort in the knowledge that one day You will reign forever in peace.

DAY 19

DANIEL AMONG PROPHETS

HIStory continues…

MICAH was another prophet to the southern kingdom of Judah. He further narrowed the identity of the coming Messiah. He prophesied the Savior would come from Bethlehem.

ZEPHANIAH foretold the destruction and restoration of the capital city of Jerusalem.

JEREMIAH prophesied boldly for forty years trying to avert the Babylonian captivity. He told Judah they would be deported to Babylon as slaves for seventy years. God had delivered His people to a bountiful country and was indeed upset with them. One day, when the Savior came, the Law of God would no longer be a list of do's and don'ts. They would follow God with their hearts. Jeremiah spoke of a new covenant that God would have with His people.

> New covenant: "Behold, the days are coming, declares the Lord, when I will make a new covenant with the house of Israel and the house of Judah,

not like the covenant that I made with their fathers on the day when I took them by the hand to bring them out of the land of Egypt, my covenant that they broke, though I was their husband, declares the Lord. For this is the covenant that I will make with the house of Israel after those days, declares the Lord: I will put my law within them, and I will write it on their hearts. And I will be their God, and they shall be my people. And no longer shall each one teach his neighbor and each his brother, saying, 'Know the Lord,' for they shall all know me, from the least of them to the greatest, declares the Lord. For I will forgive their iniquity, and I will remember their sin no more" (Jeremiah 31:31–34).

In the book called **LAMENTATIONS**, Jeremiah wrote a poem. It was full of weeping and lamenting the fall of Jerusalem and the affliction of his people, which God had allowed as judgment for its disobedience.

HABAKKUK cried to God because of the wickedness of Judah. God assured him that His judgment was coming on Judah.

And finally, the prophecies of Isaiah and the other prophets came to pass. Sadly, the Temple was destroyed, the people were captured, and they were sent to exile in Babylon. God had told the Israelites the consequences for disobedience. God had to enforce those consequences. His justice would require nothing less. The Israelites had chosen disobedience. God had been very specific in His time line and history records that the captivity lasted seventy years, exactly as was prophesied.

God sent more prophets to the people while they were in exile to comfort and reassure them that they would return to their homeland. He had to punish them, but He didn't leave them alone without His word and His hope.

DANIEL prophesied of God's protection, the restoration of His people to their land, and the promise of the future Messianic Kingdom. He gave a message of hope that some of God's people would survive. Not only did he also confirm that the time of captivity would be seventy years, but he also prophesied as to the timing of the coming of the Messiah and foretold events far in the future—specifically a second coming of the Messiah when He would be given glory and dominion over all nations. Daniel spoke of an everlasting Kingdom. Daniel, like other Old Testament figures such as Joseph and David, also gave a picture of the Savior.

Daniel's life was an example of how it's possible to faithfully obey God despite oppression. As a young man, Daniel was taken into captivity and through obedience and hard work he became an administrator in the pagan nation. There he was tempted to renounce his faith by agreeing not to pray to God and thus avoid being thrown into the lion's den. But Daniel refused to give up his habit of prayer. The king, though he favored Daniel, was forced to carry out the punishment. A merciful God closed the mouths of the lions and Daniel was spared death. Daniel, by his faithfulness in trials, was a foreshadowing of the promised Savior.

Devotional: Where Are We in HIStory?

"When Daniel knew that the document had been signed, he went to his house where he had windows in his upper chamber open toward Jerusalem. He got down on his knees three times a day and prayed and gave thanks before his God, as he had done previously." Daniel 6:10

The story doesn't tell us whether Daniel knew that God would spare his life when he entered the lion's den. Regardless, Daniel wouldn't abandon God by renouncing his practice of worship. Followers of God may still face a den of lions in the form of persecution or opposition for their faith. Our den of lions may not be physical persecution, but it may be ridicule, unpopularity, or even the loss of a job or friends. A den of lions may also be disease or death of a loved one. Remaining faithful during difficult times requires courage. How did Daniel do it? Scripture says: "He got down on his knees three times a day and prayed and gave thanks before his God, as he had done previously" (Daniel 6:10b).

Other than saying a blessing or grace at holiday dinners, prayer wasn't part of my life for a long time. It didn't occur to me that God would be able to do anything about my personal troubles. If you'd asked me if I believed in Him, I would have said yes, but I didn't know Him other than as the Creator of the universe. I likely would have laughed at the idea of praying three times a day. There was even a time I felt I was in a lion's den yet, incredibly, never turned to God.

My six-month-old daughter woke one morning staring blindly into space in a lethargic state. I rushed her to her doctor's office just up the street. He told me to take her immediately to the hospital—he thought she had meningitis. As I drove to the hospital, I remember feeling that I couldn't let her close her eyes. I had this sense that if they closed, she might never open them again. So I sang to her.

I sang every child's song I could think of: "Mary had a little lamb, little lamb, little lamb." "Bah, bah black sheep have you any wool." I sang at the top of my lungs with tears in my eyes. I sang with all the emotion I could muster. When I glanced back at her and saw that her eyes were starting to shut, I'd pick up the tempo and volume. Yet with all my passion, I never once thought to pray.

Fortunately, God had a plan for her life and she fully recovered. She was diagnosed with an unusual stomach virus that affected her blood sugar level. After ten days in the hospital, we took her home. But when I think back on that drive to the hospital, it's difficult to imagine now that I failed to pray. I missed out on the comfort and peace that God could have provided—the knowledge that He was in control.

The lesson of Daniel is not that God will always spare us, but that He will give us what we need when faced with the lions. That kind of recognition only comes from spending time with God.

Today I Pray

Lord, when I'm in my den of lions, I will commit to You—turn to You—rely on You. Thank You that You are *always* there for me.

DAY 20

THE FINAL PROPHETS

HIStory continues…

EZEKIEL prophesied to the fragments of a shattered nation. While condemning the false shepherds and priests in Jerusalem, he did offer hope by speaking of the true Messiah who would be the true Shepherd of His people.

At the end of seventy years, God's people were released from Babylonian captivity. The Lord had told Isaiah that Cyrus would restore His city and free His captive people but not for a ransom. The Persian king, Cyrus, fulfilled the prophecy only one year into his reign over Babylon. Even though Cyrus was not a Jew, God used him to free His people from the Babylonians.

After the Babylonian exile, the people were called to return to the Promised Land. They were to return to Jerusalem and rebuild the Temple, God's dwelling place. They were to restore worship. Incredibly, despite seventy years of captivity, God's people had the financial means to accomplish this due to the order of Cyrus and God's intervention.

Cyrus did more than simply free God's people. He returned all of the items stolen from the Temple when Jerusalem was captured. He also commanded the Babylonians who lived near Jewish survivors: "And let each survivor, in whatever place he sojourns, be assisted by the men of his place with silver and gold, with goods and with beasts, besides freewill offerings for the house of God that is in Jerusalem" (Ezra 1:4).

God used nations of the world to fulfill His purposes. He orchestrated the events of history to fulfill His promise to His people. He demonstrated His sovereignty again and again. Every prophecy that God gave about Israel/Judah (His people) that could have happened at this point in history had happened. The Bible records it, and the history books confirm it.

The book of **ESTHER** is another example of how God would protect His people through His divine providence. When threatened with destruction, God's people were saved through a humble and available servant—Esther.

JOEL warned Judah during a plague of locusts of another future devastation that would come if they didn't repent for their sinfulness. He saw the plague as a precursor or a picture of an even greater judgment by God on the nation. He referred to the time of future judgment as "the day of the Lord." It would be a final reckoning of sinful man with God.

God continued to send His spokesmen to Israel after they were released from exile. **EZRA,** who was a prophet and priest, led the first group of Jews back to the Promised Land.

NEHEMIAH led the second group back. He also led the people to rebuild the walls around Jerusalem for its protection.

HAGGAI moved the people to action to rebuild the Temple. His message was simple—build the Temple in order to restore the system of sacrifice and atonement. Until the Savior came, the Temple would continue to be God's provision to dwell with His people.

ZECHARIAH looked beyond the present Temple to the Messiah and the spiritual temple of God. He had many prophetic visions of the coming King and foretold that one day the King would ride on a donkey into Jerusalem: "Rejoice greatly, O daughter of Zion! Shout aloud, O daughter of Jerusalem! Behold, your king is coming to you; righteous and having salvation is he, humble and mounted on a donkey, on a colt, the foal of a donkey" (Zechariah 9:9).

And finally, the last prophet **MALACHI** cried out against the corruption of Israel. Worship and morality were once again in a state of decay. This would be God's last message for a long time. The essence of the message was for God's people to keep the Law of Moses and watch for the coming of Elijah the prophet before the great and terrible day of the Lord. And then silence. God was quiet.

The Bible doesn't record any events that transpired for the four hundred years after the prophet Malachi. History records that God's people faced horrible times, first at the hands of the Greeks and then the Romans. God's people demonstrated time and time again that they couldn't fully obey God's laws, and there were consequences for their disobedience. Does the absence of prophets or God's word mean that God was absent? Certainly not, but His timing is not ours, and history continued just as God said. Against all odds, the people of Judah were saved. God could keep His promise. Despite the oppression of many nations during the course of their history, this group of people—God's chosen—were preserved.

The Old Testament concluded, but how would the story end? Was there one from the tribe of Judah who would be born and rise as King and Savior? Would there be one who could atone for their sins and serve as a final sacrifice? Would there be one from whom the nations would be blessed? Would the promise to rid the world of Satan be kept?

Devotional: Where Are We in HIStory?

"Behold, I send my messenger, and he will prepare the way before me. And the Lord whom you seek will suddenly come to His temple; and the messenger of the covenant in whom you delight, behold, he is coming, says the Lord of hosts." Malachi 3:1

Recently, a friend shared with me a story about her son, Michael, while he was attending kindergarten at a Christian school. He was reading far above grade level. As the other students were learning their ABCs, he was already reading difficult chapter books. To keep him occupied, the teacher told him to get the Bible off the bookshelf and read that. Incredibly, he did—from cover to cover—over the course of the next several weeks. When he was finished, my friend asked him how he enjoyed it. Michael answered: "The Old Testament was exciting, Mommy, but not much happened in the New Testament." His mom laughed. Little did Michael understand at the time that all the stories of the Old Testament—the creation of the world, the flood, the promise to Abraham, the Exodus and the history of Israel, are all part of the same incredible story that reaches its climax in the New Testament when the Hero comes to save all men and women. What could be more exciting than that!

It's important to read and understand the Old Testament. It gives us the promise of the Savior. It gives us the reason why He needed to come. It gives us forecasters to predict when He would come, from what lineage, from where He would come, and how He would save. We're then able to link all of that information with the Messiah whose birth is recorded in the New Testament. This evidence will help us believe with faith that He is, in fact, the Savior and King—the central figure in God's story.

Today I Pray

Lord, thank You for giving us Your Word. Help me to read it with the mind of a child—seeing it as an exciting story that You have written for me.

Day 21

CHRIST IS BORN

HIStory continues…

Malachi, the last prophet, spoke of one who would come before the Savior. "Behold, I send my messenger, and he will prepare the way before me" (Malachi 3:1a). Now four hundred years later, John the Baptist was born to Elizabeth. His father, Zechariah, was filled with the Holy Spirit and announced that John the Baptist would "…go before the Lord to prepare his ways, to give knowledge of salvation to his people in the forgiveness of their sins" (Luke 1:76–77). John the Baptist would preach repentance and prepare the hearts of his listeners to receive the coming Savior, just as it was foretold.

Then one day, an angel of God visited a young woman named Mary. The angel told Mary she would bear a son, that he would be called Jesus, and that He would be great and would be called the Son of the Most High. Mary wondered how this could be? She was a virgin and had not yet married Joseph. The angel answered her: "…The Holy

Spirit will come upon you, and the power of the Most High will overshadow you..." (Luke 1:35).

The prophet Isaiah made the declaration that the long-awaited Savior had to be born of a virgin. This was one of the first evidentiary requirements. But the Savior had to be born of a virgin for another reason as well. Since the time of the sin of Adam and Eve, offspring were born in the image of man, not of God. The image of God had been scarred by sin. In order for the Messiah to save the world and take on the sin of humankind, He Himself would have to be without sin. He'd have to be unblemished and couldn't have a sin nature. He had to be born of a virgin. Mary—blessed among women—was chosen to give birth to this child. In faith, she proclaimed: "...Behold, I am the servant of the Lord; let it be to me according to your word" (Luke 1:38a).

A decree had gone out from Caesar Augustus requiring all newborns to be registered in the town of their lineage. Joseph, Mary's betrothed, was from the lineage of David, the tribe of Judah, and the city of Bethlehem. As the baby's birth was approaching, Mary and Joseph traveled from their home in Nazareth to Bethlehem to register in accordance with the decree.

> And while they were there, the time came for her to give birth. And she gave birth to her firstborn son and wrapped him in swaddling cloths and laid him in a manger, because there was no place for them in the inn. (Luke 2:6–7)

Remarkably, many events transpired and came together so that Jesus was born in the little town of Bethlehem in fulfillment of the Scriptures. A thousand years previously, a promise had been made to David that through his lineage he would reign forever. Hope had been vanishing, patience had waned, but then a child was born. There were shepherds out in the field. An angel appeared to them, and God's glory shone around them.

> And the angel said to them, "Fear not, for behold, I bring you good news of great joy that will be for all the people. For unto you is born this day in the city of David a Savior, who is Christ the Lord. And this will be a sign for you: you will find a baby wrapped in swaddling cloths and lying in a manger." And suddenly there was with the angel a multitude of the heavenly host praising God and saying, "Glory to God in the highest, and on earth peace among those with whom he is pleased!" (Luke 2:10–14)

After thousands of years of waiting, but in God's perfect timing, the Savior had been born.

Devotional: Where Are We in HIStory?

"…I bring you good news of great joy that will be for all the people." Luke 2:10b

When I gave birth to our first child, Ben, it was good news for my husband, for me, and for our family and friends. The rest of the world didn't care. Ben's birth had no impact on their lives. This is the reality of most births. Why then was the birth of the child of Mary and Joseph good news for *all* people? Why did this birth have an impact beyond immediate family? The answer was simple. The child born was not like any other child born in this world: "For unto you is born this day in the city of David a Savior, who is Christ the Lord" (Luke 2:11).

During the time period surrounding the birth of Jesus, there was a barrage of bad news. Even without the worldwide media of today, people were aware of the atrocities around them. The Romans oppressed the Jews, and their own king, Herod, was wicked. And yet in the midst of all this, the angel could declare that there was *good news*! The birth of Jesus was good news for *all* people.

The baby Jesus was Savior. The baby Jesus was Christ. The baby Jesus was Lord. He was and is God with us. Through God's love and humility, He came to us *as one of us*. Other religions of the world try to reach God through their own resources and works. But the Bible records that God came to us. That is the best news of all. That is news worth celebrating. Nothing has been the same since.

Today I Pray

Lord, it's with a grateful heart that I proclaim—Hallelujah! Christ is born! I am in awe that You came to us. I pray that each and every day I will be reminded of this miracle.

Day 22

JESUS THE KING

HIStory continues…

We know about Jesus's birth, life, ministry, death, and resurrection through the four gospel accounts of Matthew, Mark, Luke, and John. Each speaks to a different audience, and by this, we know the Good News that the Savior had come for all—Jews and Gentiles. While there are four gospel accounts from four different men, there are no inconsistencies. While each gospel adds different details to the story—none conflict. This is important. If the stories were identical, it would be evidence of a conspiracy. It's by their differences we know they're true.

MATTHEW's audience was Jewish. He knew that the focus of his evidence had to be related to the kingship of the Savior for the prophets had spoken of the coming Jewish king. Matthew's Gospel included evidence that Jesus fulfilled the required kingly lineage. The people had kept genealogical records in the Temple so the promised

Savior could be linked to the tribe of Judah. Matthew gives the lineage of Jesus back through Abraham.

Not only was the Savior's lineage predicted and that He would be born in Bethlehem, but it was prophesied that "...a star shall come out of Jacob, and a scepter shall rise out of Israel..." (Numbers 24:17). After Jesus was born, "...wise men from the east came to Jerusalem, saying, "...Where is he who has been born king of the Jews? For we saw his star when it rose and have come to worship him" (Matthew 2:1–2). They weren't Jewish, and yet the wise men somehow knew the promises given by the prophets, including the one regarding the celestial announcement. They saw the star and made the connection between the star and the King.

Isaiah foretold there would be homage for the coming King from foreign nations and they would bear gold and incense. And indeed, these wise men from the east who came to worship Jesus as King offered Him gifts of gold, frankincense, and myrrh.

It was also prophesied that the Messiah would be rejected and despised by many (Isaiah 49:7; 53:3, Daniel 9:26). From the time of His birth, there were reactions of hostility. King Herod wanted the baby Jesus killed. Herod was an evil man who was threatened by the coming of this alleged new King. Herod ordered that all the male children in Bethlehem be killed. History records that Herod had already killed his wife and sons, so why not this baby and the other babies in Bethlehem? An angel forewarned Joseph of Herod's plot. Joseph took Jesus and Mary to Egypt to protect them. After Herod died, an angel again appeared to Joseph instructing him to take Jesus and Mary to Israel. They went to live in the city of Nazareth.

At this time in history the Jews, under Roman authority, wanted a political king who would free them from their oppression. The Israelites' history of kings demonstrated that no human king could rescue them. The physical kingdom of Israel continually fell to more powerful nations as they could not obey the Law of God. A different kind of kingdom was needed and a different kind of king. Matthew wanted to force his readers to see Jesus as The King and worship Him as the Magi did. And Matthew's Gospel records the proclamations of Jesus that would define His Kingdom. It wouldn't be a political kingdom. Jesus came first to establish a spiritual kingdom on earth. The Kingdom of Jesus Christ would be one where:

> Blessed are the poor in spirit, for theirs is the kingdom of heaven.
> Blessed are those who mourn, for they shall be comforted.
> Blessed are the meek, for they shall inherit the earth.
> Blessed are those who hunger and thirst for righteousness, for they shall be satisfied.
> Blessed are the merciful, for they shall receive mercy.
> Blessed are the pure in heart, for they shall see God.

Blessed are the peacemakers, for they shall be called sons of God.

Blessed are those who are persecuted for righteousness sake, for theirs is the kingdom of heaven.

Blessed are you when others revile you and persecute you and utter all kinds of evil against you falsely on my account. Rejoice and be glad, for your reward is great in heaven, for so they persecuted the prophets who were before you. (Matthew 5:3–12)

Throughout the gospel accounts, the authors record the many instances where Jesus was rejected and despised, just as foretold by the prophets. They also record the prophecies that Jesus fulfilled in His birth and life. Despite all this evidence, He was not the kind of king the religious leaders wanted, so unlike the Magi, they failed to worship Him.

Devotional: Where Are We in HIStory?

"Where is he who has been born king of the Jews?…" Matthew 2:2a

The Magi boldly went to the reigning King Herod and asked, "Where is he who has been born king of the Jews?" This isn't the sort of question you want to ask a king in general, but definitely *not* Herod. Essentially, they told Herod there was one worthy of their worship—the real King!

While the Magi worshiped Jesus as King and Herod and Jewish religious leaders rejected Him, there was a third reaction to Jesus's birth. It was simply—indifference. The chief priests and scribes represented this group. They heard that the King was born, and rather than go with the Magi, they did nothing. They were not interested.

Is it really possible to be aware of Jesus and yet be indifferent to Him? Of course it is! I knew about Jesus. I celebrated His birth every December 25. But I celebrated Him as I might any other great historical figure. I had access to a Bible. I could have read the prophecies and studied the evidence. I fell in that category of those who heard about Jesus but had little interest in finding the King—finding my King.

The Magi, with no training in messianic prophecies, traveled 1,000 miles for the exclusive purpose of recognizing Jesus as King and *worshiping* Him. They saw a configuration in the heavens that indicated that a King as no other had been born, and they sought Him. They followed the light. There's a light that still leads us to the King. His Word is available to us in the Bible. But we must have a desire, as the Magi did, to seek Jesus and to put Him on the throne each and every day of our lives.

Today I Pray

Lord, You came to reign as King. I have the desire—grant me the will—to make You my KING every day of my life.

Day 23

JESUS PERFORMS MIRACLES

HIStory continues…

MARK recorded the ministry of Jesus to show that He had come as a Servant/Messiah of the people. He highlighted the teachings of Jesus to demonstrate that Jesus came to call all to follow Him as a disciple. **LUKE** recorded how Jesus was the universal savior who came to save not only the Israelites but also the gentiles of the world. He presented a very orderly account of Jesus's life and teachings for the stated purpose "that you may have certainty concerning the things you have been taught" (Luke 1:4). Each of the gospels records those events of Jesus's life and ministry, specifically the miracles that He performed, which authenticate the claim that He was the promised Messiah and King.

There are approximately thirty-five separate miracles recorded in the different gospels. They showed that Jesus had power and authority over every aspect of the physical realm—the forces of nature, life, and even death. Jesus's first miracle demonstrated His control over nature. He turned water into wine. Thereafter, He fed 5,000 men with five loaves of bread and two fish. He calmed a storm that threatened the lives of His disciples. He caught a multitude of fish after the professional fishermen had failed. With each miracle, the disciples and followers were forced to ask themselves who Jesus was. How could a mere man do these things? "What sort of man is this, that even winds and sea obey him?" (Matthew 8:27).

Jesus also had control over lives as demonstrated when He healed all kinds of sickness. Sometimes He healed by His touch and sometimes by merely His word. For instance, once a Roman centurion sent elders to Jesus in humility and faith to heal his servant: "…Lord, do not trouble yourself, for I am not worthy to have you come under my roof. Therefore I did not presume to come to you. But say the word, and let my servant be healed" (Luke 7:6–7). Jesus, amazed at this gentile's faith to believe in His authority while also acknowledging that he did not deserve anything from Jesus, healed the servant by merely His word.

Jesus showed compassion for the hurting and marginalized in His midst. Jesus healed blindness, deafness, paralysis, fever, shriveled limbs, hemorrhaging, and leprosy. Even death was subject to His authority. Jesus raised a widow's son, the daughter of Jairus, and Lazarus, after he had been in the ground for three days.

Despite the power Jesus displayed, there were many who questioned His authority. The religious leaders didn't want to believe that Jesus was the promised Messiah. They had a privileged position in the Roman world, and they didn't want that changed. They were threatened by the following that Jesus had amassed and, therefore, wanted to end His ministry. If they could find Him guilty of violating the law, they could stop Him. Doing work on the Sabbath was forbidden, so when Jesus healed a blind man on the Sabbath, they thought they'd finally "caught" Him. All they would need was the testimony of someone to state that Jesus had violated the law. Filled with prejudice, malice, and ignorance, they attempted to intimidate the healed man into stating that Jesus committed a sin—violating the Sabbath. The previously blind man's answer was simple, direct, and dismissed their accusation: He answered, "Whether he is a sinner I do not know. One thing I do know, that though I was blind, now I see" (John 9:25). Undeterred by the opposition, Jesus continued with His miracles and His teachings.

By demonstrating His power over the physical realm, Jesus authenticated His authority over the spiritual. If He could heal and raise the dead, He could certainly forgive sins. Jesus presented His reasoning to the religious scribes in an account in Mark. The gospel records that some men came to Jesus with a paralytic to be healed. With great effort to approach Jesus, they removed the roof above Him, made an opening, and lowered the bed of the paralytic. "And when Jesus saw their faith, he said to the paralytic, 'Son, your sins are forgiven'" (Mark 2:5). The scribes accused Jesus of blaspheming God, for who but God could forgive sins. In response, Jesus said to them: "…Why do you question these things in your hearts? Which is easier, to say to the paralytic, 'Your sins are forgiven,' or to say, 'Rise, take up your bed and walk'? But that you may know that the Son of Man has authority on earth to forgive sins—he said to the paralytic—'I say to you, rise, pick up your bed, and go home'" (Mark 2:8–11). If Jesus could forgive sins, wasn't He claiming and authenticating that He was indeed the promised Savior!

Matthew, Mark, Luke, and John recorded these events not merely to provide a biography of Jesus, but to encourage us to have faith in Him as the Messiah and King. For the gospel writers, Jesus was the Messiah who came not only to heal and deliver but also to suffer and die for people's sins.

Devotional: Where Are We in HIStory?

"On that day, when evening had come, he said to them, 'Let us go across to the other side.' And leaving the crowd, they took him with them in the boat, just as he was. And other boats were with him. And a great windstorm arose, and the waves were breaking into the boat, so that the boat was already filling. But he was in the stern, asleep on the cushion. And they woke him and said to him, 'Teacher, do you not care that we are perishing?' And he awoke and rebuked

the wind and said to the sea, 'Peace! Be still!' And the wind ceased, and there was a great calm. He said to them, 'Why are you so afraid? Have you still no faith?' And they were filled with great fear and said to one another, 'Who then is this, that even the wind and the sea obey him?'" Mark 4:35–41

At the time of the storm recorded in Mark 4:35–41, the disciples should have had enough knowledge of Jesus to not be worried about their lives in the boat. After all, Jesus had performed miracles in their presence. Mark records that there were other boats on the sea that day, but there was a big difference between those boats and the one the disciples were on—Jesus was on their boat! And yet they acted no differently than if He had not been with them. No wonder Jesus questioned their faith. But why did they let their fear take over? While I can only speculate, I've wondered if it has anything to do with the question that they asked Jesus: "Teacher, do you not care that we are perishing?" (Mark 4:38b). Perhaps they needed assurance that Jesus cared about them individually.

I understand that kind of doubt. I never had a hard time believing in God as the Creator of the universe. But believing that He personally cared for my destiny and me was harder to grasp.

Does God care that I'm writing this book?

Does God care that I've high cholesterol?

Does God care that I've circled the block three times to find a parking space to go to church?

I love, however, that before Jesus questioned their faith, He rebuked the wind and calmed the storm. By doing this, He not only demonstrated His authority over nature, but He showed them that He cared about their individual lives.

Over and over again, Jesus's miracles demonstrated His love and compassion for those around Him. He didn't just come to save "the world," but each individual in the world—that includes you and me.

Today I Pray

Lord, release me from any doubt that I don't matter to You. I pray for the faith to know You are always on my boat.

Day 24

GREAT I AM

HIStory continues…

In the Gospel of **JOHN**, he says there are many miracles performed in the presence of the disciples that aren't included in his accounts, but that he does highlight seven as signs of the deity of Jesus Christ: "But these are written so that you may believe that Jesus is the Christ, the Son of God, and that by believing you may have life in his name" (John 20:31).

One of the other evidences John laid out was the reaction to Jesus. Did those around Him know that He was claiming to be God? On one occasion, Jesus declared, "I and the Father are one" (John 10:30). The religious leaders were ready to stone Him right then for committing blasphemy. They knew He was claiming to be God. "…It is not for a good work that we are going to stone you but for blasphemy, because you, being a man, make yourself God" (John 10:33).

Moreover, Jesus claimed to be God by using for Him, the name that God used for Himself—"I AM." If you'll recall, in the Old Testament book of Exodus, Moses encountered a burning bush in the middle of the wilderness while sheep herding for his father-in-law, Jethro. The voice of God spoke to him out of the fire, giving him a mission to free the Israelites from bondage in Egypt. Moses asked for a sign to give the people when they challenged him: Then Moses said to God, "If I come to the people of Israel and say to them, 'The God of your fathers has sent me to you,' and they ask me, 'What is his name?' what shall I say to them?" God said to Moses, "I AM WHO I AM." And he said, "Say this to the people of Israel, 'I AM has sent me to you'" (Exodus 3:13–14).

The Jewish people knew that God's divine name was "I AM." If anyone used that name, he was either claiming to be God Himself or blaspheming God. In John's Gospel, he records the seven times that Jesus used this very name, I AM.

Jesus is claiming to be God in the flesh when He says:

> I AM the Bread of Life. (John 6:35)
> I AM the Light of the World. (John 8:12)
> I AM the Door. (John 10:9)
> I AM the Good Shepherd. (John 10:11)
> I AM the Resurrection and the Life. (John 11:25)
> I AM the Way, the Truth and the Life. (John 14:6)
> I AM the Vine. (John 15:5)

Jesus didn't have to say, "I am God" for those around Him to know that was exactly what He was claiming. Anyone who heard these declarations would know Jesus was claiming to be God in the flesh.

Devotional: Where Are We in HIStory?

"…But who do you say that I am?" Mark 8:29

After avoiding church for several years, my husband and I finally settled on one with teaching that was straight from the Bible.

Up until that time, I'd believed in Jesus as a good teacher, perhaps a rabbi, or even a prophet. I looked at Him as I would any other great man that I admired. If I followed His teachings, He could give me guidance to live as a good person—to feed the poor and show compassion. But I'd never thought of Him as someone who could change me into a new creation. Could He remove my shame for sins I'd committed in my young adulthood? Could He comfort me when I felt lonely or fearful for my children? That would require that He be more. That would require that He be God.

I wanted to be changed. If that meant studying all the evidence proving that He is the Son of God, I was willing to do that work. I began to read my Bible. I studied the claims that Jesus was more than a great teacher or prophet. Jesus claimed to be God. Everyone at the time He lived on earth knew this was His claim. I had to reach a decision. As C. S. Lewis observed: "You can shut him up for a fool, you can spit at him and kill him as a demon or you can fall at his feet and call him Lord and God, but let us not come with any patronizing nonsense about his being a great human teacher. He has not left that open to us. He did not intend to" (C. S. Lewis, *Mere Christianity*, 1942, 1943, 1944, 1952).

Today I Pray

Lord Jesus, I lift up my eyes to You today and see You not just as a teacher, a rabbi, or prophet—but also as God.

DAY 25

JESUS IS CRUCIFIED

HIStory continues…

The unconditional covenant given to Abraham had been for *a people*, *a land*, and *a blessing*. In the story, it was now time for the beginning of the fulfillment of the last promise to Abraham—that there would be a *blessing* for the nations of the world. Through the death of the Savior on the cross, the atonement for our sins would be borne by our Hero.

Jesus was arrested at about midnight in the Garden of Gethsemane, and He was tried six times in only twelve hours before both the religious leaders and the Romans. During His trials, there were at least twenty-seven violations of procedural law. In the religious court, Jesus answered, "I am" to the question, "Are you the Christ, the Son of the Blessed?" (Mark 14:61b). He was charged with blasphemy for claiming to be God. The religious leaders, however, had no authority to execute, so they brought Jesus to the Roman officials. In the Roman court, Jesus was charged with sedition. Each trial was a mockery. They had no official charges or witnesses.

The people yelled, "Crucify Him!" After all, He didn't "look" like the promised king. He didn't "sound" like a king since He was silent when accused. Of course, the prophecies had also said that He would be silent: "He was oppressed, and he was afflicted, yet he opened not his mouth; like a lamb that is led to the slaughter, and like a sheep that before its shearers is silent, so he opened not his mouth" (Isaiah 53:7). He was a man without sin, was never found guilty at law, but went to His death as a criminal.

When God substituted the animal for Isaac outside of what would become Jerusalem, Abraham had named the place "God will provide" because He knew God would provide the sacrifice. The sinfulness of the descendants of Abraham would not stand in the way of God's promise to provide a sacrifice so that we don't have to die and be separated from God.

For Jesus to be the sacrifice, however, He would have to shed His blood on Passover. Since the time of Moses, Israel celebrated how God had saved His people. Each year in Jerusalem, they sacrificed a lamb as atonement for their sins. They offered a sacrifice at 3:00 in the afternoon before Shabbat and the Feast of Unleavened Bread. On the exact hour of the last sacrifice on Passover, Jesus died on the cross; God had put meticulous care into His plan of redemption. His Son became the sacrifice.

There was physical evidence that the separation between God and man was now removed. The veil in the Temple that separated man from God was physically torn in two from top to bottom at the moment of His death. No longer would a priest be needed to intercede for us with God. We could approach the Father ourselves. Jesus became our intercessor and our perfect high priest.

The events of Jesus's life and death were fulfillments ✳ of the Old Testament prophecies regarding the promised Savior. He was of the promised lineage; His coming was announced by someone—John the Baptist—who called the people to repentance; He fulfilled the promised birth; and He fulfilled in His life what the prophets had said. During the three years of His adult ministry, Jesus demonstrated His authority as the Son of God through signs and miracles, and He continually spoke about His Kingdom. Finally, in His trial and death, many more of the prophetic words were fulfilled. For example, Isaiah spoke of a suffering servant, many of the prophets talked of a sacrifice, and God, Himself, had said that the serpent would bruise His heel. There would be injury to the promised Savior.

Christ was the perfect final sacrifice. He was innocent. The Bible and history have not recorded one sin that Jesus ever committed. He was God's unblemished Lamb, so He could take on the sins of the world so we could be set free from sin. And the nations—those that believe—are blessed. Hanging on the cross at Calvary, Jesus declared, "It is finished." The sacrifice was made. He died for us, once and for all. By not saving Himself, Jesus became the blood offering. What greater love is there?

Devotional: Where Are We in HIStory?

"So they took Jesus, and he went out, bearing his own cross, to the place called the Place of a Skull, which in Aramaic is called Golgotha. There they crucified him, and with him two others, one on either side, and Jesus between them…When Jesus had received the sour wine, he said, 'It is finished,' and he bowed His head and gave up His spirit." John 19:16–18, 30

This was such a violent and bloody death. Why? At Golgotha, most wondered why, if He is King, He couldn't save Himself? Through reading the Bible, we see God carried out His plan perfectly, including allowing for many illegal tribunals, the conviction of Jesus, and His death. Jesus had gone into Jerusalem knowing exactly what would happen to Him. He knew He was sent to die. He could have saved Himself, but then the plan wouldn't have been carried out. But again, why the cross? Why such a bloody death?

Before I came to fully believe that Jesus was my Savior, my two toddlers had been attending preschool at a local church. One morning at home, I was busy cleaning up and they were quietly playing with a set of blocks on the floor. My four-year-old son said, "Look, we made a cross!" My daughter, three, replied in the saddest voice, "Jesus died on the cross." Without missing a beat, my son said, "It's okay, He died so we could live."

I was astonished, to say the least. It gave me new perspective on the phrase, "out of the mouths of babes!" While they may have been merely repeating something they'd heard at school, I knew that it had not only somehow rung true for them, but that I was meant to hear what they said. I knew I had to decide what the cross meant to me.

The cross forces us to make a decision. There's no evidence in the Bible or elsewhere that Jesus was guilty of any crime or had ever sinned. If we accept that He died on the cross while He was innocent, we have to ask why? The Scripture also records that He gave up His spirit at the moment of death. He chose to die, just as He chose to enter Jerusalem knowing what He would face. Again, why? The only way it makes sense is if He intended to present Himself as a blood sacrifice for sin, and because He was without sin, the sacrifice wasn't for Him. Then whose sin? The cross forced me to look at myself and ask whether I'm a sinner. Was it for me that He died? Was it for you too? Was it for all of us?

Acknowledging that Jesus is my promised Savior requires that I recognize I've separated myself from God due to my sin and I need redemption. God's holiness requires perfection and I'll always fall short. It requires that I admit my need for God's grace and accept that this story was written for me.

Today I Pray

Lord Jesus, I acknowledge I am a sinner. I am eternally grateful that You bore the cross for my sins.

DAY 26

JESUS IS RISEN

HIStory continues…

The story of the Savior doesn't end with His death on the cross. If it did, we wouldn't have proof of a blessing, nor would we have the assurance of eternal life.

The Gospel of John tells us that on the third day after the crucifixion, the women who had been with Jesus returned to the tomb. There they found the stone—that had once covered the entrance—had rolled away. The body of Jesus was gone. They were perplexed. The stone was massive and couldn't have rolled away on its own. Could men have come, removed the stone, and stolen the body of Jesus? This was highly improbable in light of the historical fact that the Romans would have carefully guarded the tomb. And would the apostles have had the courage to steal His body? The apostles had already shown themselves to be very fearful. Peter had denied Jesus three times, and only John was at the crucifixion. Would these same men have confronted armed Romans to steal a body? Again, this seems very improbable. The word spread quickly that the tomb was empty. To counter the claim of the resurrection, all someone had to do was produce a body. No one could. Additionally, Jesus's burial cloths were left neatly folded inside the empty tomb. It's hard to imagine that grave robbers would have taken the time to fold the clothes. So where was the body? Two angels appeared to the women with the answer: "…Why do you seek the living among the dead? He is not here, but has risen. Remember how He told you, while he was still in Galilee, that the Son of Man must be delivered into the hands of sinful men and be crucified and on the third day rise" (Luke 24:5–7).

The empty tomb was just one piece of evidence that Jesus had risen from the dead. He appeared in His resurrected body to hundreds of eyewitnesses. More than five hundred eyewitnesses saw the risen Christ at the same time (1 Corinthians 15:6). Could this many people have had the same hallucination at the same time? Of further significance is the fact that some of the recorded witnesses were women. During this time in history, the testimony of women wasn't allowed in court. Ancient writers, if they were making up the story, wouldn't have included women as witnesses.

The evidence of the truth of the resurrection is supported by the radical change in Jesus's followers. Before Jesus died on the cross, no one was willing to defend this Savior. The followers denied him, and many yelled, "Crucify Him, Crucify Him." The apostles hid behind locked doors. Yet after witnessing the resurrection, many were willing to die for Him. What happened? What changed their attitudes? Only one answer could explain such a radical change—they had witnessed His power over death. They knew He had risen. While it's true that people through history have died for a lie, no one dies for what they *know* is a lie. Had it been a lie, the apostles and others would have known. Where was the body? Historical accounts record that ten of the original apostles died as martyrs for Jesus, as did the Apostle Paul. Since that time, countless others have died believing that the resurrection is a historical fact.

Had Jesus stayed in the ground, we'd have no proof of the blessing promised to Abraham. God's plan was for man and woman to bear witness to the resurrection to know that it was true. Jesus demonstrated His power over death. Knowledge of this fact can give us the assurance that we, too, can experience eternal life if we believe in Him and in His story. While the Savior's heel was bruised, He was not destroyed. He lives.

Devotional: Where Are We in HIStory?

"For God so loved the world, that he gave his only Son, that whoever believes in him should not perish but have eternal life." John 3:16

I was a lawyer. Much of my work was in litigation, which involves finding facts to support an argument. It was all about evidence. In law, there are different standards of proof. In many criminal cases, there must be proof beyond all reasonable doubt in order to convict. In tort or civil litigation, a case must be proved by a preponderance of the evidence or by clear and convincing evidence.

How much proof did I need to believe in the resurrection of Jesus Christ? I wasn't an eyewitness, so I had to weigh the evidence. I had to determine whether I had enough to believe even if I didn't understand all the why's and how's. Ultimately, I made the decision to believe that Jesus had indeed risen from the dead. Interestingly, once I made the decision, I knew without a doubt it was true.

I don't understand it completely, and yet I have confidence that I've been forgiven. There was a time in my life when I was filled with guilt over sin and trying to earn my way into fellowship with God. I had no understanding of His unconditional forgiveness and love for me. But when I made the decision to believe that I could receive His blessing, I felt a peace that I've never felt before. That peace has been my greatest evidence. The empty tomb became the source of my hope.

While the cross calls us to make a decision as to whether we're in need of a Savior because of our sin, the resurrection demonstrates that Jesus accomplished what was planned from the beginning. We can be forgiven and reconciled with a Holy God. We can experience the blessing promised to Abraham.

Today I Pray

Lord Jesus, I celebrate that through Your resurrection, I have assurance of eternal life. Today, as I pray, I will get down on my knees and pray with a grateful heart.

Day 27

SPREADING THE GOSPEL

HIStory continues…

After the resurrection, Jesus appeared to witnesses for forty days before He ascended into heaven. Before His ascension, however, He gave instructions to His followers: "Go therefore and make disciples of all nations, baptizing them in the name of the Father and of the Son and of the Holy Spirit, teaching them to observe all that I have commanded you. And behold, I am with you always, to the end of the age" (Matthew 28:19–20).

God's plan was that the gospel message would spread through the witness of His followers. In this way, the nations of the world would be blessed. The book of **ACTS** records the growth of the early church after Jesus's ascension. It would have seemed a daunting task—to spread to the world the message of hope and the forgiveness of sins, but He also promised them power through the Holy Spirit: "But you will receive power when the Holy Spirit has come upon you, and you will be my witnesses in Jerusalem and in all Judea and Samaria, and to the end of the earth" (Acts 1:8).

Through the power of God's Spirit, the apostles spread the message of the forgiveness of sins. God equipped the early apostles with the ability to perform miracles in order to demonstrate their authority as His witnesses. Peter healed a lame man at the Temple. Stephen performed "great wonders and signs among the people." Philip, while proclaiming the news of Christ, performed many signs including healing the paralyzed.

The church grew despite seemingly insurmountable obstacles—persecution, prison, and even death of the apostles. Nothing could thwart the growth of the church. Lives were transformed by God's Spirit, and many were baptized in the name of Christ.

God also used an unlikely individual for His purposes of spreading the gospel. Saul was a Pharisee (a Jew who strictly adhered to the Law of Moses) from the tribe of Benjamin. He studied under a famous rabbi named Gamaliel and had rejected Christ as the promised Messiah. Because of his zealous beliefs, he was part of those who persecuted the early Christians: "But Saul was ravaging the church, and entering house after house, he dragged off men and women and committed them to prison" (Acts 8:3).

One day, Saul was traveling on the road to Damascus to capture Christians and bring them back to Jerusalem to be killed. A light from heaven shone around Saul. Jesus spoke to him: "…Saul, Saul, why are you persecuting me?" (Acts 9:4). Saul acknowledged that the voice was that of the Lord, and his life was changed. Blinded by the light of the Lord, he followed the Lord's instructions to go see a man named Ananias. Ananias laid hands on Saul; Saul received the Holy Spirit and regained his sight. From that day on, Saul boldly proclaimed Jesus as the Son of God, and his name was changed to Paul. He completely surrendered his life to the Messiah and King.

Paul was given the authority to witness to the world. God's eternal Kingdom began to grow one heart at a time as the gospel spread from Jerusalem to Judea and to Samaria. Paul had three separate missionary journeys, which took him through Asia Minor and Greece. Once a man who persecuted others, Paul received persecution. He was beaten and imprisoned, but he persevered to spread the gospel. At the end of the third journey, Paul was arrested in Caesarea. How then did the gospel get to "the end of the earth?"

Paul knew the Word had to get to Rome, which was the center of the world at the time. There wasn't a single population group that Rome didn't conquer or trade with. If the Roman government could be reached with the gospel, it would be possible to reach "the end of the earth." Standing before the Jewish tribunal, Paul gave a strong defense of the gospel, told of his conversion, and concluded with an appeal to Caesar. He knew if this appeal was granted, he'd be sent to Rome. King Agrippa handed Paul over to a Roman centurion and Paul was discharged to Rome for trial. During the voyage, they encountered a storm and shipwreck, and at times, it seemed that Paul wouldn't get to his destination. But he was promised by an angel of God that he'd be tried in Rome: "… Do not be afraid, Paul; you must stand before Caesar…" (Acts 27:24).

God fulfilled His promise to Paul, and the narrative of the early church appropriately ends with Paul in Rome. As a faithful follower of Christ, Paul "…welcomed all who came to him, proclaiming the kingdom of God and teaching about the Lord Jesus Christ with all boldness and without hindrance" (Acts 28:30–31). The gospel began to spread to the end of the earth.

Devotional: Where Are We in HIStory?

*"Now those who were scattered went about
preaching the word."* Acts 8:4

One of the early martyrs was Apostle Stephen. He was stoned to death for proclaiming the Gospel of Jesus Christ. Boldly, he criticized those who refused to see that Christ was the promised Messiah of the Jews. He even called them "stiff-necked people." That event began a great persecution of the believers in Jerusalem. Many followers had to leave Jerusalem and were scattered around the world. I wonder if there were followers who wished Stephen had kept his mouth quiet and not been so vocal? Did they think many lives could have been spared if he had? But the apostles themselves didn't see the persecution as an end to their witnessing. While forced to leave, they faithfully took the Word of God with them. God used the persecution for His purpose of spreading the gospel beyond Jerusalem: "Now those who were scattered because of the persecution that arose over Stephen traveled as far as Phoenicia and Cyprus and Antioch…" (Acts 11:19).

God didn't cause the persecution of His early followers—that was the result of evil men—but He was glorified as the church grew. Evil men couldn't stop God's plan. And Stephen's boldness was rewarded in heaven: "But he, full of the Holy Spirit, gazed into heaven and saw the glory of God, and Jesus standing at the right hand of God" (Acts 7:55).

What are we willing to endure for Christ in this world? While few of us will face the kind of physical persecution the apostles faced, are we willing to endure ridicule or mocking for the sake of His Name? To this day, the key to the spread of the gospel is that there are those willing to go beyond their borders and take the message of the forgiveness of sins to the world.

God wants us to look at our circumstances as opportunities to tell others about Jesus, the promised Savior. Sometimes, He moves us to a new area. Sometimes, He opens a new job opportunity. Sometimes, He gives us a new neighbor. And sometimes, He allows hardship in our lives as He did with the early apostles. We can start stepping outside our comfort zone with baby steps, if need be. Also, we can let the example of the way we live our lives reflect the reason for our hope. As followers of Christ, we're called to be His witnesses to the end of the earth. Then one day, we, too, will see Jesus standing at the right hand of God.

Today I Pray

Lord Jesus, today I proclaim that I want to be a follower of Christ. I pray my life will be a witness to Your glory.

Day 28

LETTERS OF PAUL

HIStory continues…

Throughout Paul's journeys, as well as during times of imprisonment, he maintained contact with the churches he established. Paul's letters include **I and II THESSALONIANS, I and II CORINTHIANS, EPHESIANS, PHILIPPIANS, COLOSSIANS, GALATIANS, ROMANS, PHILEMON, I and II TIMOTHY** and **TITUS**. His letters proclaimed the gospel, encouraged the early Christians, but also corrected false teaching.

Because many of the early believers were Jewish, they wanted to keep the Old Testament dietary laws, as well as circumcision, as proof of their faith so they might be saved. Paul's teachings established that it was by faith alone that we are saved. The law's purpose was to point to our sinfulness. If we need to keep the law perfectly to come into God's presence, we would all fall short: "For by grace you have been saved through faith. And this is not your own doing; it is the gift of God, not a result of works, so that no one may boast" (Ephesians 2:8–9).

The question arose, however, could people freely sin because they were forgiven? Paul explained that they'd been set free from sin. For those who believe that Jesus Christ is the Son of God and our Savior, His Spirit comes and dwells within them. The hearts of believers become permanent "spiritual" temples for His presence. This was in fulfillment of God's promise through the prophet, Ezekiel: "And I will give you a new heart, and a new spirit I will put within you…" (Ezekiel 36:26).

This new heart and Spirit of God would direct believers to live righteously. As believers listen and obey the promptings of that Spirit, there would be a natural outpouring of God's attributes. "But the fruit of the Spirit is love, joy, peace, patience, kindness, goodness, faithfulness, gentleness, self-control; against such things there is no law. And those who belong to Christ Jesus have crucified the flesh with its passions and desires" (Galatians 5:22–24).

We see in the books of the New Testament that the Spirit of God transformed lives, giving them boldness and the ability to persevere. These writings, inspired by God, continue to be God's Word to us. Paul's letters demonstrate how we're called to live according to God's original intention—reflecting His image, worshiping Him alone, and making Him ruler over our lives.

Devotional: Where Are We in HIStory?

"Or do you not know that your body is a temple of the Holy Spirit within you, whom you have from God..." I Cor. 6:19

Recently, I was invited to a baby shower for a lovely young woman of deep faith. The attendees were each asked to write and bring a prayer for the new mother-to-be. I reflected on my own children and the prayers that I had for them once I came to believe in Jesus Christ as my Savior. What did I want for them? Certainly, I wanted them to be healthy, but what else? This was the letter I wrote:

Dear Friend,

Sometime ago, I did a study on the Temple that Solomon built. The amount of gold that was used was priceless. Certainly, Solomon spared no expense, not even on the inside where only the high priest would see.

"And Solomon overlaid the inside of the house with pure gold, and he drew chains of gold across, in front of the inner sanctuary, and overlaid it with gold. And he overlaid the whole house with gold, until all the house was finished. Also the whole altar that belonged to the inner sanctuary he overlaid with gold." I Kings 6:21–22.

Why? I learned that gold was a symbol of God's glory, and the Temple was designated as the place that God would meet His people. I then realized that it was more than appropriate that the inside would have to be as glorious as the outside. It would have to be a place worthy of God's presence.

As I was raising my children, it was very easy to fall into the trap of caring mostly for the "outside" of my children—making sure they had the right education, were involved in the right activities, and they behaved appropriately for others to see. While these were all good things, we know that God looks at the inside. Investing in those "inner" qualities that glorify God matter most. While ultimately all our children have to make their own choice to let Jesus into their hearts to dwell, every truth we speak to them, every prayer we lift up for them, prepares their bodies to be that gold-laid sanctuary. It's never time lost, and all the other things will get done.

I pray for your wisdom and discernment as you help prepare your child's heart to be overlaid with the gold of God's glory, so that the fruits of God's Spirit will be evident in her life.

Blessings,
Carole

God wants each heart to be a gold-ladened sanctuary no matter our age or circumstance. It's a lifelong process of refining our inner temple to be a glorious reflection of Him.

Today I Pray

Lord, is my own heart a fitting temple for Your glory? Help me reflect Your attributes of love, joy, peace, patience, kindness, goodness, faithfulness, gentleness, and self-control.

Day 29

BODY OF BELIEVERS

HIStory continues…

Practical instructions to the early church include the letters of **JAMES, I and II PETER, I, II, and III JOHN**, and **JUDE**. They also wrote letters to the followers of the Savior instructing each to persevere in the faith, to live as Christ lived, as a servant—loving and caring for others. They supported Jesus's own instructions: "A new commandment I give to you, that you love one another: just as I have loved you, you also are to love one another" (John 13:34). We, too, are called to "love one another" today.

All of the New Testament is meant to instruct us. It continues to be God's Word to every follower of Christ: "But be doers of the word, and not hearers only, deceiving yourselves" (James 1:22). What is written in the Bible is only part of God's story. We have the opportunity to write the continuation of God's story of blessing and salvation for the world. God has included us in His story, and we have a part to play. This means that as His followers, we can continue to spread the message of the gospel as we testify to the world.

One of the last letters in the New Testament was to the **HEBREWS**. The author wanted to remind us that we should put our faith in Christ alone. He is the greatest rescuer, for He is the Son of God; He is the greatest High Priest, for although tempted, He is without sin and can sympathize with our weaknesses; He brings a better covenant, for it is by His grace that we receive its benefits; and He is the perfect sacrifice for the atonement for sins, for His death on the cross was once and for all. As we write His story with our lives, we are exhorted to be intentional about our faith.

First, we are told: "Let us draw near with a true heart in full assurance of faith, with our hearts sprinkled clean from an evil conscience and our bodies washed with pure water." This is not a one-time event. Every day, we have the opportunity to come into the presence of God. Then, we are told: "Let us hold fast the confession of our hope without wavering, for he who promised is faithful" (Hebrews 10:23). By remembering that God has delivered on every one of His promises, we can finally: "And let us consider how to stir up one another to love and good works, not neglecting to meet together, as is the habit of some, but encouraging one another, and all the more as you see the Day drawing near" (Hebrews 10:24–25).

While each individual must make his or her own decision to believe that Christ was the promised Savior, as followers, we are part of a body of believers. We become part of God's family: "But to all who did receive him, who believed in his name, he gave the right to become children of God, who were born, not of blood nor of the will of the flesh nor of the will of man, but of God" (John 1:12–13).

When Adam and Eve sinned, their pride had prevented them from putting their faith in God. Rather, they believed the serpent's lie and essentially put their faith in themselves. When we put our faith in Christ, we become His witnesses, joining others throughout the ages to advance His Kingdom here on earth.

Devotional: Where Are We in HIStory?

"First of all, then, I urge that supplications, prayers, intercessions, and thanksgivings be made for all people, for kings and all who are in high positions, that we may lead a peaceful and quiet life, godly and dignified in every way. This is good, and it is pleasing in the sight of God our Savior, who desires all people to be saved and to come to the knowledge of the truth." 1 Timothy 2:1–4

My husband, John, was at his law office one evening working on a brief for a partner. It was getting late and he was anxious to get home for dinner. We had two active young children at the time, so I was clearly eager for him to come home and help with the evening duties. He called to explain a predicament he was in. He still had a few hours of work to do but a young associate, Ralph, had just come into his office to chat. He looked at the Bible on John's desk and asked John if he believed in "this stuff." John had answered that he did, and Ralph said he'd like to talk about it some day. After Ralph left the room, John was bothered. He had this sense that he should talk to Ralph that night, but he knew he also had the brief to finish, and he wanted to get home. John assumed that I'd assure him there would be another time to talk with Ralph, and he should get home as soon as possible.

For some reason, the words out of my mouth weren't typical of my response when John was running late. I said: "The law is your vocation, the Lord is your life." To this day, it seems an unusual thing for me to say, particularly in light of my desire to get John home for the evening.

John hung up, put his brief away, and called Ralph back into his office. For the next hour, John told Ralph about the gospel and how Jesus was the promised Savior. He explained that believing that Jesus died, as the sacrifice for our sins, was the only thing necessary to inherit eternal life. Ralph indicated that he understood and left the office to go home. Shortly after, John's partner called to tell him that he didn't need to finish the brief—they'd been granted a postponement. It was a Friday, and John left the office, grateful that he'd done what he was called to do. He felt that God blessed him for his obedience by granting the postponement.

The following Monday, John returned to work. He immediately called me with news. Ralph had been found dead in his apartment Friday evening. He was twenty-six years old. The cause of death was heart failure, though Ralph had no prior history of heart disease.

It is Jesus's desire that we testify as to who He is. That's not always an easy thing to do, and there is no question it takes a willingness to be bold as well as obedient. It's a privilege, however, to be used by God for His purposes and His story.

While we don't know if Ralph came to believe in Christ that evening, we do know that God gave Him a chance in his last hours to receive the gift of eternal life. If John hadn't been the one to witness, however, perhaps someone else would have been used for His purposes: "who desires all people to be saved and to come to the knowledge of the truth" (1 Timothy 2:4).

Today I Pray

Lord Jesus, open my eyes to see the very person You want me to tell Your story to. Give me the wisdom and discernment I need. Help me to share with compassion and love.

DAY 30

BOOK OF REVELATION

HIStory continues…

Jesus came to reconcile us to God and to invite us to enter into eternal life. People ask—if Jesus came, why do we still have war, famine, disease, and evil? At times, it feels as though Satan is winning. There is more to the story, however, that's been written but not yet realized. Jesus wants *all* to choose life, so He waits to come again. Jesus will return and usher in His eternal and peaceful Kingdom. Jesus's death and resurrection assured us of eternal life, but the ultimate destruction of Satan and all evil will take place in the future.

The story of what will happen is written in the book of **REVELATION**. While in exile on the island of Patmos, the Apostle John was given the Revelation of Jesus Christ by His angel. John bore witness to the Word of God and was instructed to write down the things that would take place in the future.

John received the Revelation in a series of visions. The events he recorded are signs and symbols of what will transpire rather than a chronology of specific events. No one knows with certainty how and when the events will take place, but these things are assured:

Christ will come again.

He will reign forever and ever.

All will know that Jesus is King.

Every knee will bow and every tongue will confess that He is Lord!

Those who die believing in Jesus Christ as the Savior have their names written in *The Book of Life*. One day, they will reign with Christ.

> No longer will there be anything accursed, but the throne of God and of the Lamb will be in it, and his servants will worship him. They will see his face, and his name will be on their foreheads. And night will be no more. They will need no light of lamp or sun, for the Lord God will be their light, and they will reign forever and ever. (Revelation 22:3–5)

As believers, our souls immediately enter the presence of God in heaven when we die our physical death on this earth. When Jesus returns the second time, we'll be given a new spiritual body suited to live in a perfect world. God's enemies—including Satan who is the source of evil—will be conquered and thrown in the lake of fire for eternity. The old earth will pass away, and a new heaven and earth will one day be established.

> Then I saw a new heaven and a new earth, for the first heaven and the first earth had passed away, and the sea was no more. And I saw the holy city, New Jerusalem, coming down out of heaven from God, prepared as a bride adorned for her husband. And I heard a loud voice from the throne saying, "Behold, the dwelling place of God is with man. He will dwell with them, and they will be his people, and God himself will be with them as their God. He will wipe away every tear from their eyes, and death shall be no more, neither shall there be mourning, nor crying, nor pain anymore, for the former things have passed away." (Revelation 21:1–4)

Just as the doors of Noah's ark closed, there will come a time when it's too late to receive God's grace. No one knows the day or the hour when this will occur. But God is patient and He wants all to come to Him. All have a choice to spend eternity in a glorious place called heaven.

Devotional: Where Are We in HIStory?

> *"Behold, I am coming soon, bringing my recompense with me, to repay each one for what he has done. I am the Alpha and the Omega, the first and the last, the beginning and the end."* Revelation 22:12–13

I love my graduated lenses. Before I got them I had to wear one pair of glasses to correct my nearsightedness and readers to correct my farsightedness. I never could see with clarity anything in between! Also, it seemed that I never had the right glasses with me when I needed them. Now I have just one pair of glasses. They let me see up close to read my devotions. They let me see around me to see my husband's face clearly when he enters the room. They let me see in the far distance to enjoy the sunset on the horizon. Yet as helpful as these lenses are, I'm more grateful for the graduated "spiritual" lenses God has given me.

Through His Word and Spirit, I can see up close. I can examine my own heart to see where I'm falling short of His Glory. God's Word lets me see my sins. In addition to seeing up close, my spiritual lenses let me see what is around me. I can see whom to love and how to serve Him. I can see the lost and hurting individuals who need love and compassion. (But my spiritual lenses are just like my graduated lenses—if I don't put them on, I see nothing.) And through the same spiritual lenses, I can see off into the far distance. There's a glorious future where He will banish evil, and those of us who believe will live with Him for eternity.

Revelation gives us a picture of the future. It allows us to endure the trials of this world with a clear vision of a future glory. It lets us live with hope. It lets us see the continuation of His story. There's a miraculous component to His story—the Bible—when we accept in faith that God authored it.

For the Word of God is living and active, sharper than any two-edged sword, piercing to the division of soul and of spirit, of joints and of marrow, and discerning the thoughts and intentions of the heart. (Hebrews 4:12)

But just as significantly, the Bible can restore us. It lets us see His forgiveness. It removes guilt and shame, it comforts through sickness and the death of loved ones. It gives peace and brings joy. The Bible reminds us that God is always with us, and He is always faithful. The Bible has had power over my life unlike any other book on my shelves. I know that His story was written for me. I know with certainly that it was written for you as well.

Do you want spiritual lenses?

1. Do you see that God had a plan from the beginning because He knew that you'd disobey Him and sin?

2. Does this make you love Him all the more, knowing that He had a plan to reconcile you to Him?

3. Do you believe that He sent his Son to die for your sins?

You can accept His gift of love and grace. You can receive spiritual lenses. You can spend your life in a story that will never end—with the one and only Creator God and King.

Today I Pray

Lord, I believe with faith that You wrote this story for me. I know that I am in need of a Savior and that Your son, Jesus Christ, died for my sins so that I can be reconciled with You and live in Your presence for eternity. Thank you for Your gift of mercy. Help me to seek You more through prayer and reading Your Word. Surround me with other believers to encourage me in my faith journey. Guide me as I share the truth of Your promises with others.

Conclusion

The Bible, read from beginning to end, tells one complete unified story. In Genesis, God created man in His image, but due to man's sinfulness, that image was broken and a gap was created between the Holy and perfect God and man. In order to reconcile God and man, God had the entire story written from the beginning. There is one main plot—God's plan to redeem is the consistent theme of the Bible. And like any good story, the plot has a Hero, or in this case, a Savior.

Throughout the Old Testament, there are allusions to the Savior who would rescue the people from their sin. In order for us to recognize Him when He comes on the scene in the New Testament, His birthplace is identified, His mission is described, and the suffering and death He would endure as part of the rescue is forecasted. When He appears in the New Testament, everything transpires exactly as written about thousands of years earlier. The Hero, the Savior, was always there in the story even though history had not yet happened. The story of Jesus, born of a virgin in a little town called Bethlehem, was referenced in the Old Testament before history records that He *was* born of a virgin in a little town called Bethlehem.

Some ask: Could someone have constructed the ending after the fact to fit with the beginning? Really? Could Jesus have planned in utero His birth of a virgin, in the town of Bethlehem? Could He have orchestrated illegal tribunals that would convict Him? Could He have planned His persecution, the piercing of His side, a crown of thorns placed on His head? Could He have put together all the chain of events that led to His death on the cross? There are many prophecies in the Old Testament. Could one man construct his life to fulfill them all?

The unified nature of the story also argues for its authenticity as divinely inspired and written. No mere man or woman could put a book together as the Bible was and tell one seamless story. Consider these facts:

1. The Bible is composed of sixty-six books. Unlike other writings, it wasn't written in one person's lifetime, but rather, it was recorded over thousands of years, by many different individuals.

2. The Old Testament comprises thirty-nine books and describes events spanning thousands of years.

3. The human authors who recorded the individual books didn't themselves live in the same generation.

4. The New Testament history begins four hundred years after the last event recorded in the Old Testament. Therefore, the writers of the Old Testament had no way of knowing how the history would proceed beyond their deaths, and yet all transpires as they had written.

The entire story was planned from the beginning and only God could have written it. He is in control. By writing HIStory as He did, God demonstrated just how great His love for us is.

"For God so loved the world, that he gave His only Son, that whoever believes in him should not perish but have eternal life." (John 3:16)

APPENDIX

Books of the Bible

Note: As with *HIStory in 30 Days: Genesis to Revelation*, the order of the books of the Bible in the chart below are primarily chronological.

THE OLD TESTAMENT	
Genesis	In the beginning God created… Man and woman sinned God promised Abraham 1) numerous descendants 2) the Promised Land 3) blessing to the nations through his descendant A sacrifice of an innocent would atone for sins Cycle began: Sin of man/judgment/hope given
Exodus	Picture of redemption and deliverance: God rescued Israel from slavery in Egypt/He raised up Moses God gave Israel the law
Leviticus	A call to worship God/the high priest would intercede for the people
Numbers	The people grumbled/God ordained 40 years of wandering before they would enter the Promised Land with a new generation

Deuteronomy	Moses's farewell speech: He encouraged Israel to obey God and God alone
Joshua	Joshua led the people into the Promised Land/the land was portioned to the 12 tribes of Israel
Judges	God established a theocracy He would be King, but gave judges
Ruth	Story of life under the Judges/Picture of redemption
I & II Samuel	Record of Samuel who anointed the first kings of Israel Establishment of David's reign *Promise of God expanded: "When your days are over and you rest with your fathers, I will raise up your offspring to succeed you, who will come from your own body, and I will establish his kingdom"*
Psalms	Book of poetry regarding the attributes of God
Proverbs	Book of wisdom
Ecclesiastes	Account of life written by Solomon
Song of Solomon	Book of love/marriage is a gift of God and picture of God's relationship with His people
Job	God's power over Satan demonstrated Word of future redemption given: *"I know that my redeemer lives, and that in the end he will stand on the earth. And after my skin has been destroyed, yet in my flesh I will see God."*

I & II Kings	Record of the kings The Divided Kingdom established/Israel to the north and Judah to the south
I & II Chronicles	Genealogies recorded/parallel account of the kings
Prophets to the Northern Kingdom/Israel	**Message:** Warnings of Judgment
Amos	*"Prepare to meet your God"*
Hosea	Picture of forgiveness for unfaithfulness
Prophets to the Nations	**Message:** Warnings to the enemies of Israel
Obadiah	Warning to Edom
Jonah	Prophet to Nineveh
Nahum	Warning of destruction to Nineveh
Prophets to the Southern Kingdom/Judah	**Message:** Warnings of Judgment
Isaiah	Picture of future Redeemer: His birth and ministry
Micah	
Zephaniah	
Jeremiah (and his book of Lamentations)	Warning of Babylonian captivity Lament over nation's sinfulness
Habakkuk	

Prophets to the Kingdom while in Captivity	**Message:** Promises of Hope
Daniel	Promise of protection/forecast of the Messianic Kingdom
Ezekiel	
Esther	Picture of God's protection of His people in order to preserve the promise
Prophets after the release from Captivity/ Return to the Promised Land	**Message:** Rebuild the Temple
Joel	Locust invasion is a forecast of future judgment
Ezra	Priest who led first group back to Promised Land
Nehemiah	Governor who led 2nd group
Haggai	Rebuild the Temple
Zechariah	A future king promised
Malachi	The last prophet/a promise of one to come who would prepare the way for the Redeemer
THE NEW TESTAMENT	The Savior comes/the story continues with us
Matthew	Promises fulfilled—the Savior comes! Jesus is the Messiah
Mark	Jesus is the Christ, the mighty worker
Luke	Jesus is the universal Savior
John	Jesus is the Son of God

Acts	The Holy Spirit at Work: History of the early church / Experiences of Peter and Paul / "Go and make disciples"
I Thessalonians	*"Be joyful always; pray continually; give thanks in all circumstances, for this is God's will for you in Christ Jesus."*
II Thessalonians	We must persevere in the faith
I Corinthians	We have a new life in Christ / united in sound doctrine / our body is the temple of the Holy Spirit
II Corinthians	We are being transformed into His likeness
Ephesians	We are created to do good works but we are saved by grace alone
Philippians	We have joy in Christ and are to have a generous heart
Colossians	We should make Christ our Lord of all
Galatians	We have freedom in Christ
Romans	We are saved by grace
Philemon	We have brotherhood/sisterhood in Christ
I Timothy	We need to oppose false doctrine and "fight the good fight of faith"
II Timothy	We need to keep sound doctrine
Titus	We need to stand firm in the gospel of grace
James	We are given a practical letter of Kingdom living
I Peter	We should expect suffering and persecution
II Peter	We need to continue in Godly living

I John	We need to love others
II & III John	We need to beware of false doctrine
Jude	We must contend for the faith
Hebrews	We have Christ, the better sacrifice
Revelation	Eternal Hope: Evil will be destroyed. Promise of a new heaven and new earth